Palms and Cycads

David Squire

First published in 2007 by New Holland Publishers Ltd.

London • Cape Town • Sydney • Auckland

• 86 Edgware Road, London W2 2EA, United Kingdom

• 80 McKenzie Street, Cape Town 8001, South Africa

• 14 Aquatic Drive, Frenchs Forest NSW 2086, Australia

• 218 Lake Road, Northcote, Auckland, New Zealand

www.newhollandpublishers.com

ISBN (HB) 978 184537 298 9

ISBN (PB) 978 184537 300 9

Publishing Managers: Claudia Dos Santos and Simon Pooley
Commissioning Editor: Alfred LeMaitre
Editor: Roxanne Reid
Designer: Lyndall du Toit
Illustrators: Châtelaine Tayler, Bonnie Lusted
Picture Researcher: Karla Kik
Production: Myrna Collins
Proofreader/indexer: Anna Tanneberger
Consultant: Martin Gibbons

Reproduction by Resolution Colour (Pty) Ltd, Cape Town
Printed and bound by Times Offset (M) Sdn. Bhd., Malaysia
10 9 8 7 6 5 4 3 2 1

DISCLAIMER

Although the author and publishers have made every effort
to ensure that the information contained in this book was
accurate at the time of going to press, they accept no respon-
sibility for any loss, injury or inconvenience sustained by any
person using this book or following the advice given in it.

CONTENTS

Introduction

Palms and cycads often appear to be a legacy of a time when the world of plants was in its infancy, as the leaves of many of them have a fossil-like outline. Although we usually think of palms as being tall, with leaves clustered at their tops, many in fact have a clump-forming or scrambling nature. They all belong to the *Palmae* family, which encompasses approximately 200 genera and 2 600 species, although there are claims for as many as 211 genera and 2 779 species. They are mainly native to the tropics and subtropics, although a few survive warm-temperate climates.

The A–Z of palms in Chapter 5 describes and illustrates almost 100 palms; many others are described in Chapter 4.

Cycads are among the earliest seed-bearing plants and were much more common in prehistoric times than they are now. Nevertheless, the range of cycads today is still wide; it encompasses three families (*Cycadaceae, Stangeriaceae* and *Zamiaceae*), 11 genera and about 300 species. They are mainly native to tropical and subtropical areas, although some grow in warm-temperate regions. Many have a palm-like nature, with leathery leaves and woody trunks, sometimes very short.

While botanically unrelated to palms, the palm-like appearance of cycads often leads people to associate them, and many palm societies around the world incorporate a cycad component.

The A–Z of cycads in Chapter 6 describes and illustrates 18 cycads; many others are featured in Chapter 4.

THE TEMPERATURE QUESTION

Like most other plants, palms and cycads are easy to grow in their native regions, but are not always successful in foreign areas, especially those with a different and cooler climate. Tropical or subtropical temperatures are essential to many palms, although a few grow well in warm-temperate climates. In cool-temperate areas, however, many palms – and a few cycads – will grow indoors or in conservatories.

Throughout the A–Z sections in Chapters 5 and 6, indications are given of regions where these plants can be grown outdoors. For the United States, these are shown through the USA Plant Hardiness Zones, which are described in detail and indicated on a map in the Appendix (see page 152). European and Australian climates, and how these relate to the USA Zones, are also featured in the Appendix, on page 153. (For instance, gardeners in the UK should look mainly for palms that grow in USA Zones 8 and 9.)

To reiterate, these zones indicate where palms and cycads will grow outdoors. This is not to say that you must forswear growing these plants if you live in a cooler area, but you will need to grow them indoors or in a conservatory. For lists of palms suitable as houseplants or conservatory plants, see pages 31 and 32.

1

The anatomy of palms and cycads

Palms

Palms display a range of leaves (fan, feather, fishtailed or entire), trunks and differing growth styles (trunkless, clumping, solitary, even climbing).

THE NATURE OF ROOTS

Like the roots of all other land plants, those of palms form an anchor and absorb nutrients and water from the soil. During its infancy and when a seedling, a palm has a primary or seminal root system, which is short-lived. Basically, its role is to anchor the palm during its seedling stage and to absorb water and nutrients.

Palms also have a secondary set of roots that arise from the base of the trunk to form an adventitious, or supplementary, root system. The nature of this root system varies from one species to another. If the soil is fertile and moisture-retentive, it can be very small. For this reason many palms can safely be planted close to buildings or in relatively small containers. Normally, however, they penetrate the soil quite deeply, spreading and giving the trunk resistance to strong wind.

The roots of palms are usually tough and thick, although slender and wiry ones are also known. Some roots creep over the soil's surface, while a few palms even develop aerial roots that may eventually make them appear to be growing on stilts.

AERIAL ROOTS

A few palms develop aerial roots at or near the base of the trunk or stems. These include *Cryosophila warscewiczii* (Rootspine Palm) and *Clinostigma exorrhizum*, a palm native to Fiji and where wet fogs prevail.

Other palms with aerial roots include *Pinanga aristata*, *Verschaffeltia splendida* (Seychelles Stilt Palm) and *Socratea exorrhiza*. Some of these develop into stilt or prop roots, which often form a cone and give the palm extra support; they usually occur on palms native to wet soils and humid conditions, where the base of the palm is at risk from decay. Indeed, in a few instances, the lower part of the trunk withers and the palm is entirely supported by these roots.

Verschaffeltia splendida
(Seychelles Stilt Palm, Latinier Latte)

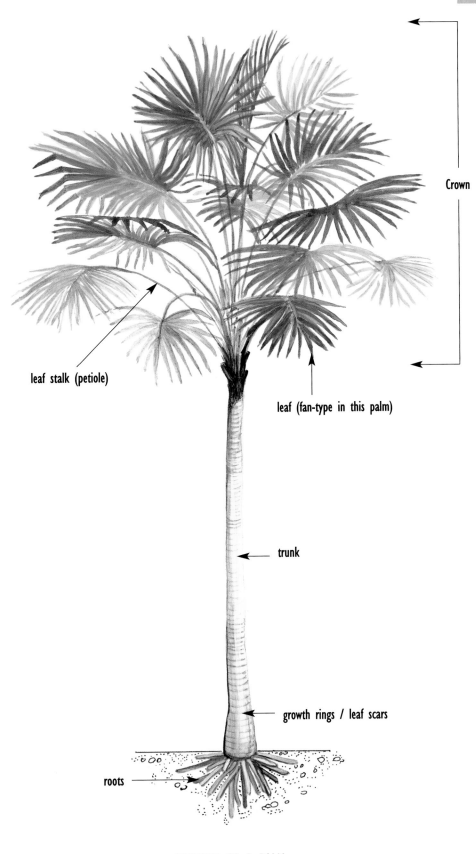

Crown

leaf stalk (petiole)

leaf (fan-type in this palm)

trunk

growth rings / leaf scars

roots

ANATOMY OF A PALM
Livistona australis (Australian Cabbage Palm)

THE NATURE OF TRUNKS

The trunks of palms essentially do not have bark as traditional trees do, but an epidermis that hardens to provide protection and some support. The trunk develops in relation to – and following – the creation and development of leaves. During a palm's early years, the developing leaves thus provide protection for the bud that creates upward growth.

Trunks vary in their diameter, most achieving their final diameter as the trunk grows; seldom does it widen as a result of later upward growth of the palm. Most trunks are straight, but a few are swollen, perhaps the best known of these being *Hyophorbe lagenicaulis* (Bottle Palm) and *Hyophorbe verschaffeltii* (Spindle Palm). The trunk of *Hyophorbe lagenicaulis* has a bulbous base, while that of *Hyophorbe verschaffeltii* is narrow at its crown and base, but widens at its centre.

Trunk surfaces vary too. Whereas some are relatively smooth, such as *Jubaea chilensis* (Chilean Wine Palm, Coquito Palm), the trunk of *Aiphanes aculeata* (Ruffle Palm, Chonta Ruro) is ringed in black spines. Some palms have a mass of fibres on their trunks, such as *Trachycarpus fortunei* (Chinese Windmill Palm, Chusan Palm).

The range of trunks includes some with distinctive growth rings (formed of scars from old leaves), such as *Howea belmoreana* (Belmore Sentry Palm, Curly Palm). *Adonidia merrillii* (Christmas Palm, Manila Palm) has indistinct growth rings, while *Phoenix roebelenii* (Dwarf Date Palm, Roebelin Palm) has dominant, persistent leaf bases.

CROWNSHAFTS

Some palms with pinnate-type leaves have crown-shafts (the upper part, where leaves spread out from the trunk). Pinnate leaves are feather-like, with leaflets growing from both sides of the central leaf-stem in a flat arrangement or at angles that create a plumose, or feather-like, effect. Genera that have species with this nature include *Archontophoenix*, *Rhopalostylis* and *Roystonea*.

Archontophoenix

The crownshaft is usually bright green, although in some species of *Pinanga* it is yellow. With *Cyrtostachys renda* (also known as *Cyrtostachys lakka*, whose common names include Sealing Wax Palm or Lipstick Palm), it is waxy-red to scarlet. Most crownshafts are smooth, but some may be scaly, hairy or spiny.

Swollen trunk
Hyophorbe lagenicaulis (Bottle Palm)

Hairy trunk
Trachycarpus fortunei (Chinese Windmill Palm, Chusan Palm).

Growth rings
Jubaea chilensis (Chilean Wine Palm)

Dominant leaf bases
Phoenix roebelenii (Dwarf Date Palm)

Fan-leaved *Chamaerops humilis* (European Fan Palm)

Wedge-shaped fan leaves *Licuala spinosa* (Mangrove Fan Palm)

Feather-type leaves *Phoenix canariensis* (Canary Island Date Palm)

THE NATURE OF LEAVES

Also known as fronds, the leaves of palms have varied natures; some are borne at the top of a palm in a distinctive crown, while others have leaves on stems that develop from lower down on the trunk or even from stems that arise directly from the ground. A range of leaf shapes is discussed below.

Fan-leaved palms

Also known as Fan Palms, these have leaves with a circular or semi-circular outline. The leaves resemble fans and are either partly divided and known as palmatifid, or referred to as palmate if totally divided. The leaf divisions are known as segments.

Palms with fan-shaped leaves include *Chamaerops humilis* (European Fan Palm, Mediterranean Fan Palm), *Trachycarpus fortunei* (Chinese Windmill Palm, Chusan Palm) and *Washingtonia filifera* (Californian Fan Palm, Petticoat Palm).

Licuala spinosa (Mangrove Fan Palm, Spiny Licuala) has wedge-shaped leaflets.

Feather-type palms

Also known as Pinnate Palms, these palms have fronds that are divided on either side of the mid-rib, with the impression of many leaflets. They are sometimes described as the 'backbone and ribs of a fish'.

Palms that reveal this style include *Howea belmoreana* (Belmore Sentry Palm or Curly Palm), *Howea forsteriana* (Kentia Palm or Thatch Leaf Palm) and *Lytocaryum weddellianum* (Dwarf Coconut Palm, or Weddel Palm).

The leaflets, also known as pinnae, are variable in size, shape and the angle at which they are attached to the central leaf-stem, or rachis. Some arise from the rachis in a flat, even formation, such as *Archontophoenix alexandrae* (Alex Palm, Northern Bangalow Palm) and *Archontophoenix cunninghamiana* (Piccabeen Bangalow Palm). Some, such as *Howea belmoreana* (Belmore Sentry Palm, Curly Palm),

Feather-type leaves *Howea belmoreana* (Belmore Sentry Palm)

Fishtail palms

Also known as bipinnate palms, these have leaves that are twice divided and have a fishtail appearance at their tips. Examples are *Caryota mitis* (Clustered Fishtail Palm, Tufted Fishtail Palm) and *Caryota urens* (Fishtail Palm, Toddy Palm).

Entire-leaved palms

These attractive palms are unusual in that the leaves are undivided in their mature state. One example of this type is *Johannesteijsmannia altifrons* (Diamond Joey).

create an angled, upright, perhaps V-shaped formation, while others droop. Some have leaflets in two distinct planes, such as *Phoenix canariensis* (Canary Island Date Palm), while others have an uneven distribution along the rachis, including the beautiful and popular *Hydriastele wendlandiana* (Florence Falls Palm, Latrum Palm).

A further type has a plumose (feather-like) and irregular arrangement of leaflets, such as *Syagrus romanzoffiana* (Giriba Palm, Queen Palm).

Fishtail-type *Caryota urens* (Fishtail Palm, Toddy Palm)

Entire-leaf type *Johannesteijsmannia altifrons* (Diamond Joey)

THE NATURE OF GROWTH

Palms have a wide range of growth habits, from those that are trunkless to those with a clumping nature, or majestic palms with tall trunks. Some even have a climbing nature.

Trunkless palms

Several palms appear to be trunkless, including those that later form dominant trunks but, while young, seem to have only a mass of leafstalks growing from low down on the palm and from ground level. Often, palms native to scrubby land or dense forests are trunkless.

A few palms have trunks that are wholly or partly beneath the soil's surface, including *Sabal minor* (Blue Palmetto Palm, Little Blue Stem) and *Serenoa repens* (Saw Palmetto, Scrub Palmetto).

Clumping palms

As the name suggests, these palms have multiple trunks or stems. They include popular species such as *Dypsis lutescens* (Golden Cane Palm, Yellow Bamboo Palm), *Phoenix dactylifera* (Date Palm, Date) and *Phoenix reclinata* (African Date Palm, Senegal Date Palm).

Sometimes, a clump of palms is initially formed of many stems, but later one or two become dominant and much larger, forming trunks (such as *Chamaerops humilis*). When some clump-forming palms are grown as ornamental features, shoots at the base of the plant are removed to produce a single trunk with a dominant, uncluttered nature. As a result, it is sometimes difficult to identify a palm that should have a clump-forming nature, but does not appear to do so.

Solitary palms

To most people, these are the epitome of palms, especially when seen on an idyllic desert island. Palms with solitary trunks include *Adonidia merrillii* (Christmas Palm, Manila Palm), *Livistona australis* (Australian Cabbage Palm, Gippsland Palm), *Phoenicophorium borsigianum* (Latanier Palm), *Trachycarpus fortunei* (Chinese Windmill Palm, Chusan Palm) and *Washingtonia filifera* (Californian Fan Palm, Petticoat Palm).

Branching palms

Few palms have a natural branching nature although branching can sometimes occur as the result of damage to the growing point of a trunk. *Hyphaene thebaica* (Gingerbread Palm) is native to northern and northeast Africa, where it has a natural, freely branching and clustering nature. *Serenoa repens* (Saw Palmetto, Scrub Palmetto) is a trunkless palm with lateral underground stems that send up new stems.

Trunkless palm
Sabal minor (Blue Palmetto Palm)

Clumping palm
Dypsis lutescens (Golden Cane Palm)

Solitary trunk
Washingtonia filifera (Californian Fan Palm)

Branching palm
Hyphaene thebaica (Gingerbread Palm)

Climbing palms

More than 600 palms have a climbing nature, including *Calamus australis* (Lawyer Cane, Rattan Palm), with its scrambling, climbing, clustering nature and stems that are up to 25m (80ft) high in the wild.

Many palms with a climbing nature initially form clumps, with stems usually known as canes; a few have a single climbing stem. Occasionally, the canes spread over the ground until they find a plant to which they can cling. Many climbing palms have canes clothed in spines and hooks. These enable them to cling to a host, and give it protection from animals. The clusters of flowers also aid in supporting canes, as many have spine-like hooks.

Climbing palm *Calamus australis* (Lawyer Cane, Rattan Palm)

THE NATURE OF FLOWERS

The arrangement of flowers (inflorescences) in palms varies widely, including those at the tops of stems that grow from ground level and those in the heads or crowns of palms.

Palms flower when they are mature and this varies from one palm to another. Palms with a relatively low stature flower earlier in their lives than tall types. For example, *Chamaedorea elegans* (Good Luck Palm, Parlour Palm), which grows up to 3m (10ft) high and is often grown as an indoor palm, may flower when four to six years old, whereas *Lodoicea maldivica* (Double Coconut, Seychelles Nut), which can be 25m (80ft) or more in the wild, can be 40 or more years old when it bears flowers.

Some palms are termed monocarpic, indicating that a stem or trunk dies once it has borne flowers. Unless the palm has a clumping nature or is formed of many individual stems, it results in death of the entire plant.

Axillary inflorescence
Caryota urens (Fishtail Palm) dies after flowering.

Several palms produce their flowers terminally and towards the top of a trunk, whereas others develop axillary inflorescences from shoots at the junctions of leaf-stalks or just below the crownshaft of palms with pinnate (feather-like) leaves.

terminal inflorescence

axillary inflorescence

The individual flowers of palms are usually small and are borne in clusters that sometimes bear more than a million individual flowers. Some are attractively fragrant, such as *Coccothrinax fragrans* (Fragrant Cuban Thatch, Yuraguana) and *Hyophorbe verschaffeltii* (Spindle Palm), while others like *Arenga pinnata* (Sugar Palm, Gomuti Palm) have drooping clusters of purple flowers with a rather unpleasant aroma.

Some palms have flowers that have a bisexual nature, with both male and female parts present. They are called hermaphrodites. Others have a unisexual nature, with only one sex present. Unisexual flowers can either be borne separately on the same inflorescence, or in separate inflorescences on the same palm. Finally, many species have male and female flowers on separate plants.

Unlike many flowers on trees, those on palms are relatively short-lived and usually last for only about a day. They are either pollinated by insects, such as honeybees, flies and beetles, or by the wind.

THE NATURE OF FRUITS

Palm fruits and seeds vary in size and colour. They are botanically either a drupe (fleshy and usually with a single stone-like seed, like a plum or cherry) or single-seeded berries. Many palm fruits are edible and succulent, perhaps the best known being *Phoenix dactylifera* (Date Palm), which has been part of the diet of millions of people for centuries, especially in warm regions.

Edible fruit *Phoenix dactylifera* (Date Palm)

Edible fruit *Cocos nucifera* (Coconut Palm)

Cycads

Cycads have distinctive natures, with a range of leaves, leaflets, stems and roots, as well as cones. Most grow in soil at ground level but a few, such as *Zamia pseudoparasitica*, have an epiphytic nature and grow attached to trees. They are not parasitic and just use their host for support.

Epiphytic cycad

THE NATURE OF ROOTS

Cycad seedlings have taproots and sometimes develop a contractile nature that helps to anchor the plant in the ground. The structure of roots is variable, and depends on whether the cycad's stem is subterranean (beneath the ground) or arborescent (tree-like). Cycads that have subterranean stems tend to have tuberous, succulent roots that can store water and nutrients. In arborescent cycads, plants slowly lose the taproot, replacing it with a spreading root system that serves to anchor the cycad and absorb water and nutrients from the soil. They do not have great water-storage capabilities.

Another type of root is coralloid (resembling coral in structure). These occur slightly above or fractionally below the soil's surface. They contain algae known as cyanobacteria (or blue-green algae) that can convert nitrogen in the air into nitrogenous compounds that a cycad can use. This enables cycads to exist in poor, infertile soils.

Coralloid roots
Dioön spinulosum
The brittle roots contain nitrogen-fixing cyanobacteria.

THE NATURE OF STEMS

Stems are either arborescent or subterranean. Cycads with arborescent stems are often headed by a crown of leaves. Their stems are usually unbranched, covered in old leaf-bases, and are sometimes 9m (30ft) or more high.

Cycads with subterranean stems are shorter. Whereas some have scars left by old leaf-bases (genera such as *Cycas* and *Encephalartos*), others lack scars and are tuberous (genera such as *Stangeria* and *Zamia*).

Arborescent stem *Cycas revoluta* (Japanese Fern Palm, Sago Palm)

Subterranean stem *Cycas circinalis* (False Sago, Queen Sago)

THE NATURE OF LEAVES AND LEAFLETS

Cycads have leaves that are naturally divided into two ranks of leaflets on either side of the main midrib, either opposite or alternate. Leaves range in length from 10cm (4in) to 6m (20ft). A few cycads, such as *Cycas multipinnata*, have leaves that are branched, with the secondary branches bearing leaflets.

Leaflets differ in colour and shape, while in size they range from 3cm (1¼in) long in the petite *Zamia pygmaea* from the dry hills and pinelands in Cuba, to 50cm (20in) long and 25cm (10in) wide in *Zamia wallisii*, which is native to wet and tropical rain forests in Colombia, South America.

Leaf colour ranges from yellowish-green to dark green, with some having bronze-green or purplish-green shades. With some cycads the leaflets are attached flat and horizontally to the leaf's midrib, while others are at an angle or in a V-shape, either upward or downward.

THE NATURE OF CONES AND SEEDS

Botanically and structurally, cones are formed of leaf-like structures called sporophylls, which produce spores. The cones vary in size and shape and there are both male and female types.

Cycads are dioecious, which means male and female cones are produced on separate plants. It has been known, however, for cycads to change their sex – invariably as a result of plants experiencing near-death through drought, cold, heat or physical damage.

The sizes, shapes and colours of cones are detailed for each species in Chapter 6. From the union of male and female spores, cycads produce seeds, which are ripened, fertilized ovules within the cone (botanically known as fruits). They are usually egg-shaped, although cylindrical and globular ones are known. When seeds germinate they initially produce a taproot (see The nature of roots, page 14).

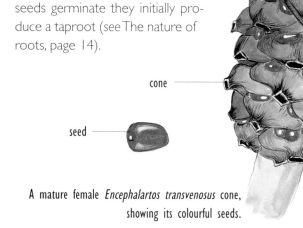

cone

seed

A mature female *Encephalartos transvenosus* cone, showing its colourful seeds.

CYCAD LEAF DIVERSITY

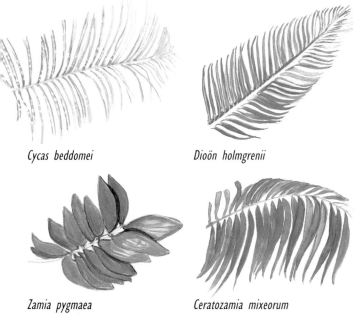

Encephalartos hirsutus

Zamia inermis

Cycas beddomei

Dioön holmgrenii

Zamia pygmaea

Ceratozamia mixeorum

Cycad cones of *Encephalartos transvenosus* (Modjadji Cycad)

2
Buying and looking after palms and cycads

Palms are bought in temperate and warm-temperate climates throughout the year to decorate homes and conservatories. They are also used ornamentally outdoors or in town planning as street and avenue trees, and in the creation of hedges, screens and groundcover (see pages 35–36), while many have a commercial value.

Cycads can be grown outdoors in warm-temperate to tropical areas (see pages 41–42), as well as in containers outdoors and as houseplants.

BUYING PALMS AND CYCADS

Always visit a reputable nursery when buying a palm or cycad and never attempt to dig one up from the wild in the hope that it can be re-established in your garden. Apart from the impracticalities of re-establishing a dug-up plant in your garden, many species are under threat in the wild, while several are extinct. Here are a few clues to buying a palm or cycad successfully.

- Buy from a reputable source to ensure plants in the wild are not being damaged.
- Look under and above leaves for signs of pests and diseases (see pages 23–25), as well as physical damage.
- Check the container is not too small and has not been constricting the roots. The roots should fill the container, but not be bursting out. The compost should be slightly moist, but not saturated.
- Ensure that the plant is labelled and has the necessary permit (see box on page 17).

THE NEED FOR PLANT PERMITS

A cage has been erected around the base of this *Encephalartos woodii* cycad to prevent people from stealing the suckers.

Many plants are protected under the Convention on International Trade of Endangered Species of Wild Fauna and Flora (CITES), signed by 80 countries in 1973. The agreement controls commercial trade in endangered plants and animals, and depredation through land clearance. Some palms, and all cycads, are protected by CITES, so check before you buy these plants that the importer has the necessary permit. Where nurseries raise plants from seeds and cuttings, this is legitimate nursery trade, though some seeds are also covered by CITES.

Such protection is necessary as many cycads and other plants across the globe have been decimated, perhaps unwittingly at first, then with determined greed and for commercial gain. Before the colonization of countries and migration of millions to foreign lands, native people lived harmoniously with plants. For example, Seminoles, members of the Muskhogean tribe of Florida, USA, used stems of *Zamia floridana* (also known as *Zamia integrifolia*) a source of starch for making bread. Settlers in Florida in the early 1800s copied them, opening the first mill to grind stems and extract starch in 1845. Such was richness of this cycad in starch (about 50%) that there was soon a large industry in producing starch, drying and packing it in barrels for shipment to northern states.

Other countries used cycads in similar ways. In the early 1920s, starch was extracted from *Macrozamia communis* native to New South Wales, Australia, while in the Dominican Republic, *Zamia pumila* was also used as a source for bread.

Decimation of cycads and other plants eventually caused alarm among botanists and environmentalists, leading to the CITES agreement.

GETTING YOUR PLANT HOME

Unless the nursery delivers the palm or cycad to you, you will invariably take it home in a car.

- Ensure that other occupants of the car – dogs and young children – cannot damage them.
- Keep plants out of strong sunlight and hot or cold draughts from open windows.

On arriving home

- Initially, put indoor plants in a lightly shaded, slightly warm position; with outdoor plants, especially in the tropics, position in the shade.
- Check the compost is slightly moist; if dry, you may need to water it several times.
- With indoor and conservatory plants, slowly acclimatize them to a change in light intensity. Light intensity in your home may be duller than in the garden centre, whereas it may be higher in a conservatory.
- Plant outdoor palms and cycads as soon as the soil is workable and not excessively wet or dry, and when the weather is not exceptionally hot or cold. Always check the climate suits the plant.

CORRECTING ACIDIC SOIL

The acidity or alkalinity of soil can be measured by using a lime-testing kit or a pH-testing meter. The latter is ideal for gardeners who are red/green colour blind.

The lime required to decrease acidity in the soil depends on the form in which it is applied and the type of soil. The following amounts decrease acidity by about 1.0 pH. With palms, aim for a pH of 6.0 to 6.5; for cycads, 7.0 is desirable but anything between 6.5 and 7.0 results in good growth.

Soil	Hydrated lime	Ground limestone
Clay	610g/m² (18oz/yd²)	810g/m² (24oz/yd²)
Loam	410g/m² (12oz/yd²)	540g/m² (16oz/yd²)
Sand	200g/m² (6oz/yd²)	270g/m² (8oz/yd²)

PLANTING A PALM OUTDOORS

Palms in the wild grow in a wide range of soils (*see* Chapter 5 for preferences). However, most grow in fertile, well-drained but moisture-retentive soil, with a pH of 6.0 to 6.5. The logarithmic pH scale measures acidity or alkalinity in a range from 1.0 to 14.0, with 7.0 being neutral. Figures higher than 7.0 indicate increasing alkalinity; lower ones, increasing acidity.

The pH of acid soils can be corrected; the amount of either hydrated lime (calcium hydroxide, also known as slaked lime) or ground limestone (calcium carbonate ground to a fine powder) needed depends on the nature of the soil (*see* box on page 17). However, reducing the alkalinity of soil – which makes it difficult for plants to absorb elements such as iron, magnesium, manganese and zinc – is more difficult. Success mainly involves selecting palms that grow in alkaline conditions, such as *Brahea armata, Butia capitata, Chamaerops humilis, Phoenix canariensis, Phoenix dactylifera, Pseudophoenix sargentii, Sabal minor, Sabal palmetto, Syagrus romanzoffiana, Washingtonia filifera* and *Washingtonia robusta*.

If the soil is light and sandy, it may not retain sufficient moisture during hot weather, so mix well-decomposed farmyard manure or garden compost into the soil before planting.

Soils with high clay content are usually richer in plant foods than sandy types, but are not well drained and aerated, so growth is retarded. With such soils, mix in copious amounts of sharp sand (also known as concreting sand) and well-decomposed farmyard manure or garden compost. Also, install land drains if water does not drain readily.

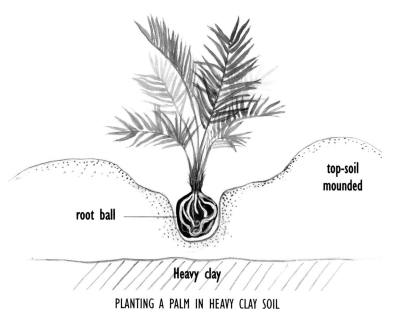

PLANTING A PALM IN HEAVY CLAY SOIL

PLANTING A PALM IN WELL-DRAINED SOIL

Step-by-step
Planting a palm outdoors

Late spring and early summer are the best times to plant palms outdoors.

1. Prepare the soil several months before planting, removing roots of perennial weeds and mixing in bulky organic materials such as well-decomposed farmyard manure or garden compost. If preparation time is limited, at least ensure all parts of perennial weeds have been removed. Dig the soil to a depth of 30cm (12in), breaking up large pieces. Mix in well-decomposed garden compost. Peat can be added, but is usually slightly acid so may make the soil too acid if used in large amounts.

2. A month or two before planting, test the soil's pH; if needed, dust the soil surface with hydrated lime or ground limestone. Later, lightly fork it into the surface soil.

3. The day before planting, water the compost in the container several times. Also water the planting area without causing waterlogging; allow the surface to dry slightly before planting.

4. Prepare the planting site by digging a hole large enough to accommodate the root-ball, then form and firm a sligt mound in the hole's base.

5. Where the area is predominantly clay and badly drained, mound the soil to form a raised area (*see* left) instead of positioning the root-ball so that its surface is level or fractionally below the surrounding area. Firm the soil, then dig out the planting hole.

6. If the soil is well drained, dig a hole large enough to accommodate the root-ball (*see* above).

7. Carefully remove the root-ball from the container and position it in the hole. If the main viewing position of the plant is from a specific direction, rotate the root-ball until the palm's best side is towards that area.

8. Place a straight strip of wood across the planting area and check that the surface of the root-ball is fractionally below the surrounding soil (see right).

9. Carefully draw friable (crumbly) soil around the root-ball and firm it in layers. Use the heel of your shoe to ensure it is firm. Afterwards, shallowly rake the surface level to prevent water resting in puddles. Thoroughly but gently water the entire area. Ensure the palm is labelled with its name and planting date.

10. Spread a layer of well-decayed farmyard manure or garden compost 7.5cm (3in) thick over the planting area, but not touching the trunk. This helps to conserve moisture in the soil and provides food for the palm.

use a straight plank to check levels

CHECKING THE PLANTING DEPTH

Step-by-step
Transferring a palm into a larger container

Palms dislike root disturbance and only need to be repotted when their roots completely fill the pot. This may be every two or three years – or longer. Essentially, be guided by the density of the roots.

1. The day before repotting a palm, water its compost several times; allow excess to drain.

2. Select a clay or plastic pot slightly larger than the present one. Clay pots are usually better than plastic: they have greater rigidity and keep the compost cooler as excess moisture can readily percolate through their sides. Place a few broken pieces of clay pots in the base to ensure good drainage.

3. Loam-based compost, such as a mixture of loam, sharp sand and peat, is ideal for palms, as it provides a firm base. Place a few handfuls in the new pot.

4. Carefully remove the root-ball from the container without damaging the roots and place in the new pot. Its surface should be about 12mm (½in) below the rim for a pot about 10–13cm (4–5in) wide and up to 25mm (1in) for a pot 25cm (10in) wide. This ensures there is plenty of space for water to rest in the brim when the plant is watered.

5. Carefully firm compost around the root-ball – in layers rather than all at once. Add a label to the pot and thoroughly but carefully water the compost without disturbing the surface compost unduly.

Water the root-ball the day before transferring the palm to the bigger pot.

Be careful not to damage the roots.

PLANTING A CYCAD OUTDOORS

Large cycads are more difficult to move successfully than small ones, and take longer to become established. Well-drained soil is essential and light loams and sandy gravels are best. Avoid heavy, badly drained clay soils, which encourage root decay. Clay soils can be improved by mixing in copious amounts of sharp sand or clean gravel, while exceptionally light soils that retain little moisture can be improved by incorporating some well-decomposed farmyard manure or garden compost.

Like palms, cycads will grow in a range of soil pH. A pH of 7.0 (chemically neutral) is best, but anything between 6.5 and 7.0 produces good results. (See box on page 17 for how to correct excessive acidity.)

Step-by-step
Planting a cycad outdoors

This is best tackled during spring and early summer and usually involves transferring a container-grown plant to its garden position.

1. Prepare the soil several months earlier, removing roots of perennial weeds and adding bulky well-decomposed manure or sharp sand. If preparation time is limited, at least ensure all parts of perennial weeds have been removed. Dig the soil to a depth of 30cm (12in), breaking up large pieces and mix in well-decomposed garden compost.

2. Small plants transplant better than large ones; most cycads are small when planted because these are cheaper than large specimens. The day before transplanting, water the compost and allow excess to drain. Although cycads retain moisture, they need as much moisture as possible in their stems and leaves when being replanted. Lightly water the planting area without excessively saturating the soil. Allow it to dry slightly before planting.

3. On planting day, carefully remove the root-ball from the container. Where large roots are damaged, cut them back cleanly with a knife and coat with fungicide. If the cycad is large, cut back some of the foliage to reduce moisture loss from the plant.

4. Dig a hole slightly larger than the root-ball, then form and firm a slight mound in the hole's base.

5. Place the root-ball on the mound and orientate the plant so its best side is facing towards the main viewing area. Check that the top of the root-ball is slightly below the surrounding soil by placing a straight piece of wood

across the hole. In stages, return soil to the hole and firm it in layers around the root-ball.

6. When planting is complete, thoroughly soak the planting area and spread over it a layer of well-decomposed garden compost, 7.5cm (3in) thick, but not touching the stem. This helps to conserve moisture in the soil and provide some food.

7. In exposed areas, support tall cycads by placing rocks around their stems. This is less obtrusive than using stakes and wires.

CYCADS FOR CONTAINERS

Cycads are ideal for growing in containers, indoors or around houses and on patios. They also have a history of being used in bonsai. When grown indoors, select cycads that grow in low-light areas (an idea of this is given in Chapter 6 and includes, among others, species such as *Ceratozamia*). Cycads that naturally grow in areas with high light will develop long and unhealthy leaves when in shade. Also, for safety, select those that do not have sharp spines.

Cycads live for many years in the same container, although for rapid growth choose one where the roots are not constricted. Use well-drained but moisture-retentive compost. Once the cycad is established, give it a weak liquid fertilizer every four to six weeks during its growing season. Take care not to feed the plant excessively as unused fertilizers in the compost could eventually damage the roots.

Cycads can live for many years in the same container if it is large enough not to constrict the roots.

LOOKING AFTER PALMS

Mulching

Palms have shallow roots and an annual mulch of well-decomposed garden compost or farmyard manure, 7.5cm (3in) thick, helps to provide them with food and keep soil cool and moist. It also suppresses the growth of annual weeds. Other materials with an organic nature (but not providing nourishment) are bark, wood chippings and peanut shells. Sawdust is often suggested, but is not recommended as it packs down, becomes unsightly and prevents air and water entering the soil.

Inorganic materials for mulching include gravel, pebbles or black polythene (which can be covered with pebbles or bark to improve its appearance).

Before putting down mulch, preferably in spring, shallowly fork the previous organic mulch into the surface and add a dusting of fertilizer (see Feeding below); thoroughly water the soil.

Pruning

Palms require little pruning, other than removing dead fronds and the remains of clusters of fruits in spring. Take care not to damage the growing point (usually towards the top of the palm, from where growth is initiated) because the palm will die. Misplaced suckers are often removed, as are those from around naturally suckering palms when grown as solitary-trunked ornamental features. Remove large suckers by digging down and severing them with a sharp spade or knife. Those around palms in a lawn setting can often be restrained by regularly mowing over them.

Old or dead fronds are often left around palms to create an unusual, attractive feature, but they eventually encourage vermin and are potential fire hazards. Long-handled shears or a stepladder may be required, but ensure that it is held securely by a friend.

Feeding

Palms are gross feeders and respond to regular applications of fertilizers, especially those with high nitrogen content. In spring and before applying mulch, dust the soil with a high-nitrogen fertilizer. Apply a balanced fertilizer two or three months later, and another in the early part of late summer. In temperate climates, do not feed palms late in their growing seasons they will not be able to make use of the nutrients. Apart from being a waste of money, the soil may become toxic if winter rains do not leach away excess fertilizer.

Watering

Most palms, even those that naturally grow in relatively dry soils, benefit from moist soil. Their roots spread widely, so saturate the entire area thoroughly when watering them. Water during evenings or early mornings, when the chance of water immediately evaporating is low. Do not simply dampen the surface soil. The frequency of watering depends on the soil; if light and porous, more water is needed than if it is moisture retentive.

Palms growing outdoors do not usually need to be sprayed with water, but gently spray the foliage if they are newly planted and growing in shade. Indoor palms benefit from regular misting with clean water, but not when in strong, direct sunlight in summer. Encouraging humidity around the foliage of palms indoors helps to deter red spider mites and decrease the risk of fronds becoming dry and their tips assuming dark, crisp areas.

Wind protection

Protection from strong, buffeting winds is often required when palms are newly planted and before roots are established. Erect a temporary screen by using canvas or shade cloth on the windward side, but do not restrict air circulation by encircling the plant.

Shade cloth can be used to protect a newly planted palm from wind until its roots become established.

LOOKING AFTER CYCADS

Mulching

Plants benefit from a layer of well-decomposed farmyard manure or garden compost, 7.5cm (3in) thick, spread over the soil in late spring. First remove all weeds, dust the soil with a general fertilizer and thoroughly water the entire area. Do not allow the mulch to touch the cycad's stem.

Pruning

Cycads rarely need pruning, except when damaged or outgrowing an allotted area. When transplanted, large cycads benefit from the removal of stems and foliage. This reduces the plant's need to absorb water from the soil before its roots are re-established. Use sharp, crossover-type secateurs (or long-handled types) to cut stems cleanly.

Feeding

Regular application of fertilizers makes cycads healthier and faster growing. Give several applications of fertilizer during their growing season, usually from spring to late summer, though this is influenced by climate and their natural growing season. Applications of a general fertilizer every six weeks is about right; too frequent applications can dangerously raise the concentration of salts in the soil, especially if the weather is hot and plants are not being adequately watered. Soils that have too high a concentration of salts prevent plants from absorbing moisture and nutrients from the soil.

Watering

Cycads often grow in dry soil, but growth is improved and leaf colours become brighter when given regular moisture. How often you should water depends on the soil; light, porous soils need more water than moisture-retentive soils. Thoroughly soak the complete root system at each application; never let the roots become dry. Newly planted cycads need regular watering until their roots are established.

Cycads are watered in several ways: when in pots, usually through a hosepipe, but in ornamental areas, with a sprinkler system or small pipes laid on the ground. Sometimes, mulching materials are used to cover the pipes.

Light

Cycads vary in how much light they need. This is indicated for the individual species described in Chapter 6. However, young cycads of up to about five or six years old benefit from slight shade.

PESTS OF PALMS AND CYCADS

Few palms and cycads suffer greatly from pests and diseases, although some damage does occur, especially when plants are in large groups and are insufficiently fed and watered. Some pests and diseases are specific to palms and cycads, while others are general to all plants.

The chemicals permitted by legislation vary from country to country and state to state so if prevention fails, check with your local nursery or garden centre about the most suitable insecticide or fungicide to use for your specific problem.

Aphid	Also known as Plant Lice, Greenfly or Blackfly, they pierce soft tissue and suck sap, causing debilitation and transmitting viruses from plant to plant. They excrete honeydew, which attracts ants and encourages the presence of Sooty Mould, a black fungus. Use an insecticide as soon as they are seen; repeated sprayings are usually necessary.	They are mostly seen on young shoots in spring, when new growth appears. They suck sap, causing distortion to the leaves and shoots. Spray several times with an insecticide.
Beetles		Several different types of beetles feed on cycads and can soon ravage both young and older leaves, especially in spring and early summer. They are often most active at night. Pick off and destroy beetles and spray with an insecticide.
Caterpillar	Several types can be troublesome, especially when plants are deprived of water. They chew the foliage and create an unsightly mess. Spray regularly with an insecticide.	Caterpillars can decimate young foliage, especially in spring. If seen, spray several times with insecticide.
Mealy Bug	These resemble small, white, wax-covered woodlice. They cluster under leaves and around junctions of stems and leaves, sucking sap and causing weakness in the plant. Dryness at the roots intensifies the problem. Small infestations on indoor palms can be eradicated by wiping them with methylated spirits or rubbing alcohol. Outdoors, as well as indoors, chemical sprays are useful.	These are similar to those that infest palms and are often seen on cycads in greenhouses or plants outdoors and in shade. Spray with oil-based sprays, but check that the foliage does not become burned.

PEST	PALMS	CYCADS
Palm Weevil	Adults are shiny, about 6cm (2½in) long and with curved snouts. They are especially damaging to *Phoenix* species and soon kill even previously healthy palms. The larvae bore into the crown and feed on soft tissue. Use an insecticide as soon as they are seen.	
Red Spider Mite	These near-microscopic, spider-like, eight-legged creatures cluster on the undersides of leaves, sucking sap and causing yellowing and mottling. Mist-spraying plants with clean water helps to deter them. Spray with an acaricide.	These cause the same damage to cycads as palms: sap is sucked, resulting in yellow, mottled areas. Regularly spray plants with clean water; also use an acaricide.
Scale Insects	Several forms attack palms indoors and outdoors in the tropics and subtropics. They feed by piercing and sucking a plant's tissue, causing debilitation. When young and at the crawler stage, scale insects are relatively easy to eradicate either by spraying with an oil-based spray (regularly check that it does not burn the foliage). For indoor plants, wipe with a cotton-bud dipped in methylated spirits or rubbing alcohol. Later, when they are protected by a scale-like housing, eradication is difficult and repeated sprays are necessary at two-week intervals with a systemic insecticide.	Like Scale Insects on palms, they are relatively easy to eradicate at the crawler stage if they are seen in time. Once they form established colonies they become more difficult to eradicate. Nevertheless, spraying three times with an oil-based spray (but taking care that the leaves are not burned) at two-week intervals will eventually eradicate them.
Thrips	Sometimes known as Thunder Flies, they are minute, elongated insects that pierce the foliage of palms, especially when young and soft. They suck sap, causing silvery mottling. Spray regularly with an insecticide.	
Whitefly	In temperate zones these are pests of greenhouse and indoor plants, but are also outdoor pests in warmer areas. They resemble small moths and, when disturbed, flutter in masses from one plant to another, sucking sap and causing debilitation and unsightliness. They excrete honeydew, which encourages the presence of ants and Sooty Mould. Spray with an insecticide; syringing with clean water helps to deter them.	

WARNING

Before using a chemical spray to control pests or diseases on palms and cycads, check with your garden centre that it is suitable. Also, if the palm or cycad is indoors, ensure that the spray is suitable for indoor use.

DISEASES OF PALMS

Bacterial Wilt

Sometimes known as Sudden Wilt, Fatal Wilt or Hartrot, this is a serious bacterial problem with Oil Palms and Coconut Palms. At first, the lower leaves turn light grey or yellow and wilt. This is followed by gummosis (gum-like secretions) on the trunk, discoloration of the vascular tissue within the trunk, and then its collapse. There is no known cure and the best preventative measure is to buy palms from a reputable source.

Bud-rot and Wilt

This is common in Coconut Palms, causing damage to young leaves and growth buds and often resulting in a palm's death. There is no known cure and the best preventative measure is to buy palms from a reputable source.

Leaf-spot

This is especially damaging to palms indoors and in conservatories, where light intensity is insufficient. It is mainly found on palms in shady areas and rarely known on plants in full sun. Small, round, yellowish and transparent spots merge into large, irregular, grey-brown blotches, which may result in the death of the plant. Use a chemical spray if seriously infected.

Lethal Yellowing

This is a serious, palm-killing problem, especially for Coconut Palms. In Florida and Jamaica it has decimated *Phoenix* species but has not spread to the Pacific region. Symptoms include the yellowing and death of young fronds in the crown, blackening of flowers, death of roots, and drooping and change of colour in older fronds. Eventually, the palm collapses and dies. There is no known cure and the best preventative measure is to buy palms from a reputable source and to spray against sap-sucking insects to prevent spread of the infection.

Palm-leaf Blight

This fungal disease infects the leaves of feather-leaved palms, causing blotches and brown spots. Sometimes, these areas merge and may be surrounded by a pale or yellowish area. Use a chemical spray if the infection is serious.

Sooty Mould

Also known as Black Smut, this fungal condition is encouraged by honeydew excreted by sap-sucking insects, such as Aphids. Although harmless, it is unsightly, and can be removed by wiping with a damp cloth. Get rid of the pests and it will disappear.

Mealy bug and scale insects

3
Increasing palms and cycads

Most gardeners buy their palms and cycads from reputable nurseries, an excellent way to prevent decimation of plants in the wild. You can also raise your own plants. Cycads can be raised by seed, offsets or cuttings, while palms are mainly increased by seed and basal offsets (sucker-like growths). Aerial and stem layering or bulbils (small bulb-like organs) can also be used, but are suitable for relatively few palms.

INCREASING PALMS

Raising palms by sowing seeds is often thought to be difficult, but apart from the technique of sowing, the prime requirement is fresh seed. This is offered through seed catalogues and by companies advertising on the Internet. Germination usually demands moist, but not waterlogged, compost and high temperatures of about 35°C (95°F). However, temperate area palms will germinate at room temperature. High humidity is essential later to prevent seedlings from shrivelling and to ensure rapid growth.

Constantly providing high temperatures requires a heated greenhouse, together with a propagation frame that provides bottom heat. Even at these high temperatures germination is not rapid, and some palm seeds, such as *Elaeis guineensis*, take three months or more. Others, such as *Washingtonia*, can germinate in a couple of weeks.

Some seeds (such as species of *Adonidia* and *Hyophorbe*) benefit from being soaked in water for a week or so before being sown; change the water every day to remove growth inhibitors leached from the seeds.

Suitable compost

Clean, pest- and disease-free, moisture-retentive compost is essential, although it should allow excess moisture to drain. Palm nurseries use mixtures of sharp sand and peat, with additions of moisture-retentive materials such as perlite and vermiculite. Sometimes, sawdust and pine bark are added.

Sowing palm seeds

Sow seeds in compost in seed-trays; evenly firm the compost, first with your fingers and then with a compost presser, to about 12mm (½in) below the rim. Avoid shallow seed-trays, which may inhibit early root development.

Systematically spread the seeds over the compost so they do not touch. Use a horticultural, flat-based sieve to spread compost over the top to a depth slightly more than the thickness of the seeds. Stand the seed-tray in a bowl shallowly filled with clean water; remove it when moisture rises to the surface, and allow excess moisture to drain.

Use a compost presser to firm the compost evenly.

Place the seed-tray in a propagation frame in a heated greenhouse, where temperatures of 35–38°C (95–100°F) can be maintained. Avoid temperatures in excess of these, which may damage the seeds of some palms. Keep the compost moist but not waterlogged.

After germination – and when the seedlings are large enough to handle – reduce the temperature slightly and transfer the seedlings of palms such as *Howea*, *Sabal* and *Washingtonia* species to small but deep, individual pots. Note, however, that some palms resent disturbance of their roots, including *Coccothrinax* and *Thrinax* species. Sow them directly into small, deep pots, or to move them from seedlings trays into to small pots while they are still small.

There are also a few palms that develop deep roots – up to 1m (3½ft) deep have been recorded – before producing a leaf and stem above ground. Clearly, these resent any root disturbance and are best sown in large, deep containers and later transferred complete with all possible compost directly into the ground. This method is only suitable in tropical or subtropical regions and involves species such as *Borassus* and *Hyphaene,* as well as *Lodoicea maldivica* (Seychelles Nut, Double Coconut).

COCONUT SEEDS

Occasionally, coconuts are offered for sale as houseplants in temperate climates, when they have about half the nut exposed and a shoot growing from the top. They are not usually successful as long-term houseplants but have great novelty value. Commercially, in the tropics, the nuts are sown – half buried in moisture-retentive but well-drained compost – in containers outdoors and in a warm, sheltered position. Later, the containers are moved to a nursery area and, later still, plants are transplanted to their growing positions (*see box on page 28*).

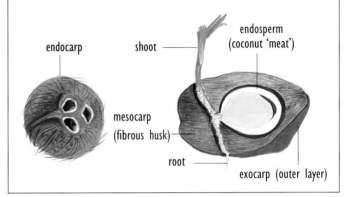

GERMINATING SEEDS IN POLYTHENE BAGS

This is an excellent space-saving method to germinate seeds of the same species without using seed-trays or pots. Mix seeds with moist peat and place in a strong, clear, polythene bag. Completely seal the bag at the top and place in a warm, shaded greenhouse, perhaps under the bench. When leaves and roots can be seen, transfer the seedlings to individual pots. Avoid strong or direct light, which will overheat the compost.

In the tropics, new plants are often raised by positioning each nut on its side in a nursery bed and partly covering it with friable soil. They need warmth and moisture, and take three to six months to germinate. In ten months each seedling, with its nut attached, can be transferred to its growing position.

An alternative method is to sow each seed where it will germinate and the plant will grow. Holes of about 90cm (3ft) square and deep are dug several months before seeds are sown, and left open to the weather. A single coconut is sown in each hole and partly covered with friable soil. During the following months, and through cultivation and weathering, soil naturally falls into holes and eventually becomes level with the surrounding ground.

When growing coconuts commercially, these holes are spaced 8.5–9m (28–30ft) apart and they provide a more secure start for the young plants than when they are germinated in a nursery bed. These holes offer young plants protection from knocks and strong winds, and the soil in the holes is likely to be more moist than when on the surface.

Raising palms from offsets

This is an excellent way to increase palms that produce offsets at their bases. Offsets are usually known as suckers. Palm species that can be increased in this way include *Chamaedorea cataractarum*, *Chamaedorea seifrizii*, *Chamaerops humilis*, *Dypsis lutescens*, *Laccospadix australasica*, *Phoenix dactylifera*, *Phoenix reclinata*, *Ptychosperma macarthurii*, *Rhapis excelsa* and *Rhapis humilis*.

Removing offsets is best undertaken in late spring or early summer. Use a spade or trowel to draw soil away from the offset. Then, use a sharp knife or saw to sever the offset, without damaging it or the parent.

Many offsets have roots, and the survival rate of those that do not is low. If you detect the lack of roots before the offset is totally severed, twist or bend it and repack soil around it. This often encourages it to develop roots, and the soil can be removed later.

After your have removed an offset with attached roots, it can be transferred to a pot for later planting, or planted directly into its growing position.

offset

INCREASING CYCADS

The sex life of cycads is more complicated than that of most garden plants, with male and female reproductive parts appearing in the form of cones on different plants. These vary: their sizes, shapes and colours are indicated in Chapter 6.

Sowing seeds

Equally complex with cycads is the time when seeds can best be sown. Whereas some cycad seeds are suitable for sowing immediately they become available, others (such as *Cycas*, *Dioön*, *Encephalartos* and *Lepidozamia* species) need several months after shedding before sowing is possible. Do not remove the seed, but allow it to fall off. Sometimes this takes a year or more.

Cycad seeds – both individual species and mixtures – are available through seed catalogues. They are also available through companies advertising on the Internet.

Sow seeds in seed-trays with well-drained but moisture-retentive compost (such as sponge rock, which is crushed volcanic rock). Do not use ordinary compost as this invariably introduces bacteria and fungal spores that are harmful to cycad seeds and seedlings. Firm the compost, first with your fingers and then with a compost presser, to 12mm (½in) below the rim. Then press each seed lengthwise into the compost, to a depth of about half its diameter. Ensure each seed is covered and spray with a fungicidal solution.

A warm temperature is essential, as well as bottom heat of about 27°C (80°F). Keep the compost evenly moist and when roots reach about 25mm (1in) long, transfer each seedling (plus the seed still attached to it) to a small, but deep pot. Again, keep the compost moist but not waterlogged; if the medium becomes dry, roots are soon damaged.

Raising cycads from offsets

Often known as suckers, offsets develop around some cycads and can be detached to produce further plants. They usually have their own roots, which ensures they become established and develop into individual plants when they are removed.

At the beginning of their growing season each year, usually late spring and early summer, use a sharp chisel or knife to sever the offset from its parent. Trim back damaged roots and dust with a general fungicide. If the offset has a lot of leafy growth, cut it back so the roots do not need to absorb so much moisture from the compost before they are fully developed. Transfer the suckers into large containers and later, when growing strongly, move them to their growing places. Avoid damaging the mother plant.

Offshoots are growing from the roots of this *Encephalartos trispinosus*.

Suckers (offsets) grow from the base of the trunk of a *Cycas revoluta*.

4

Palms and cycads for all places

Palms are mainly tropical and subtropical plants, with a few hardy enough to grow outdoors in warm-temperate regions. Some are suitable for areas with frost, and palm trunks are resilient to high winds, even cyclones. Indeed, *Cocos nucifera* (Coconut Palm), is widely seen along the coasts of South Pacific Islands, where it is the first tall plant to meet the onslaught of strong tropical winds.

Several are superb as houseplants and in conservatories – useful in cooler climates where palms do not thrive outdoors – or they make good groundcovers and hedges.

Many cycads also have a tropical and subtropical nature, but some thrive in temperate and warm-temperate climates. Some prefer full sun, others like shade; many tolerate hot and dry soils and others prefer wet and moist conditions.

HOW TO USE THIS CHAPTER
This chapter highlights palms and cycads that are suitable for specific conditions. Where the plant's name is cross-referenced to a page number in the A–Z sections, further information is available in Chapters 5 and 6, including the USA growing zone/s most suitable if the plant is outdoors (see Appendix, pages 152–153). Information on other palms and cycads not discussed in the A–Z sections is given in the tinted boxes. Note that where common names are not given, they do not appear to exist.

Palms as houseplants and in conservatories

Phoenix roebelenii

Other houseplant and conservatory palms

Calyptrocalyx micholitzii
Solitary-trunked, small palm with undivided, deep-green leaves. New leaves are purplish-orange and later assume light- and dark-green mottling. Dull to bright light suits it.

Calyptrocalyx petrickianus
Also known as *Calyptrocalyx forbesii*, this graceful palm has an erect and clump-forming nature, with feather-like green leaves, purplish-brown when young. It is ideal in a warm conservatory. Position in dull to medium light.

Chamaedorea arenbergiana
Elegant palm with a solitary dark-green trunk, 25mm (1in) in diameter, with golden-brown leaf bases and dull, deep-green leaflets that are yellowish-green beneath. Position in dull to medium light.

Chamaedorea costaricana
Costa Rican Bamboo Palm
Clumping-type palm, tall when mature but ideal for growing in a pot when young. Arching, olive-green to dull deep-green leaflets. When young, give it a shaded position, but increase the light as it grows.

Chamaedorea geonomiformis
Necklace Palm
Slender-stemmed, small palm with shiny, dark-green leaves notched at their tips. Grows best in dull to moderate light.

Chamaedorea hooperiana
Graceful, clumping and branching palm with mid- to dark-green, feather-type leaves. Grows best in lightly shaded positions; keep the compost moist.

Chamaedorea radicalis
Distinctive palm with erect and spreading, medium- to dark-green, slightly glossy and fern-like, rather sparse leaves. A relatively hardy palm; place in light shade.

Chamaedorea sartorii
This palm has a solitary, slender trunk with pinnate, mid-green leaves borne in a spreading crown. Position in dull to bright light.

Kentiopsis oliviformis
Tall and distinctive palm when mature; when juvenile, it resembles *Howea forsteriana*, with spreading, deep-green leaves. Position in light shade.

Licuala borneensis
Dwarf palm, with tufted growth and wedge-shaped, dark-green leaflets. Position in light shade, especially when young.

Licuala cordata
Dwarf, very attractive palm with a short stem and bright-green, undivided, circular to fan-shaped leaves. Position in light shade, especially when young.

Licuala ramsayi
Australian Fan Palm
Small palm with a solitary trunk and large leaves formed of mid-green, narrowly wedge-shaped segments. Position in light shade, especially when young.

Linospadix minor
Clump-forming palm, often sparsely covered with thin stems, bearing arching fronds formed of mid- to dark-green leaflets with toothed ends. Position in light shade.

Livistona robinsoniana
Solitary, slender trunk with bright-green, fan-shaped leaves that droop at their tips. Position in light shade.

Livistona rotundifolia
Footstool Palm, Round-leaf Fan Palm
It has a solitary trunk and glossy, deep-green leaves, circular when young (later, they do not form complete circles). Position in light shade, especially when young.

Ptychosperma lineare
Solitary or clump-forming, elegant palm with fronds formed of narrow, glossy, mid-green leaflets. Position in light shade, especially when young.

Rhapis multifida
Finger Palm
When young, this distinctive palm has leaves formed of five glossy, stiff, medium-green segments; mature plants have about 12 segments. Position in good light, but with light shade when young.

Rhapis subtilis
Dwarf Lady Palm, Thailand Lady Palm
Small, densely clump-forming palm with glossy, dark-green leaf segments; it resembles *Rhapis excelsa*, but has fewer leaf segments. Position in light shade, especially when young.

Rhopaloblaste augusta
Earlier known as *Ptychoraphis augusta*, this beautiful and distinctive palm has a solitary nature and a rounded head formed of long, narrow, dark-green leaflets. Position in light shade.

Rhopaloblaste elegans
This solitary-trunked palm has graceful leaves formed of light-green, narrow leaflets. Position in light shade.

Livistonia rotundiflora Footstool Palm

Palms for outdoor containers in warm regions

These palms are ideal for growing outdoors in containers on patios or terraces. They vary in their need for warmth and are therefore arranged in three groups – tropical, tropical or subtropical, and subtropical and warm-temperate.

Chamaedorea elegans

Other palms for outdoor containers
TROPICAL AND SUBTROPICAL CONDITIONS

Calyptrocalyx micholitzii
Solitary-trunked, small palm with undivided, deep-green leaves. New leaves are purplish-orange and later assume light- and dark-green mottling. Position in light shade.
USA Zones 10b and 11

Calyptrocalyx petrickianus
Also known as *Calyptrocalyx forbesii*, this graceful palm has an erect, clump-forming nature, with feather-like green leaves, purplish-brown when young. Position in light shade.
USA Zones 10b and 11

Chamaedorea brachypoda
Short-stemmed, clump-forming palm with dark-green, heavily ribbed leaflets; there are usually only a few leaves, which are nevertheless attractive. Position in light shade.
USA Zones 10b and 11

Chamaedorea geonomiformis
Necklace Palm
Slender-stemmed, small palm with shiny, dark-green leaves notched at their tips. Grows best in dull to moderate light.
USA Zones 10 and 11

Licuala cordata
Dwarf, attractive palm with short stem and bright-green, undivided, circular to fan-shaped leaves. Position in light shade, especially when young.
USA Zones 10b and 11

Licuala glabra
This is a small, solitary-stemmed palm with nearly circular leaves that have wedge-shaped, dark-green segments. Position in light shade.
USA Zones 10b and 11

Licuala ramsayi
Australian Fan Palm
This small palm has a solitary trunk and large leaves that are formed of bright-green, narrowly wedge-shaped segments. Position in good light.
USA Zones 10b and 11

Licuala rumphii
Celebes Fan Palm
Has a dense, clumping nature and semi-circular, dark-green fronds with up to 10 wedge-shaped leaflets. Position in light shade.
USA Zones 10b and 11

Linospadix minor
Clump-forming palm, often sparsely covered with thin stems bearing arching fronds formed of mid- to dark-green leaflets with toothed ends. Position in light shade.
USA Zones 10 and 11

Livistona rotundifolia
Footstool Palm, Round-leaf Fan Palm, Serdang
This attractive palm has a solitary trunk and glossy, deep-green leaves, circular when young. Later, they do not form complete circles. Position in light shade when young.
USA Zones 10b and 11

Reinhardtia latisecta

Pinanga copelandii
Beautiful palm with solitary stem and dark-green leaflets with slightly indented tips. Grows best in light shade.
USA Zones 10 and 11

Pinanga densiflora
Clump-forming palm with colourful foliage; becomes bluish-green and patterned with brown and green as it matures. Position in light shade.
USA Zones 10 and 11

Pinanga disticha
Small, clustering palm with shiny brown stems and dark-green, narrow leaflets marbled with paler spots and blotches. Position in light shade.
USA Zones 10 and 11

Ptychosperma lineare
Solitary or clump-forming, elegant palm with spreading fronds bearing narrow, mid-green leaflets. Position in full sun or light shade.
USA Zones 10 and 11

Ptychosperma microcarpum
Solitary or clump-forming and clustering palm with light-green leaflets. Position in full sun or light shade.
USA Zones 10 and 11

Reinhardtia latisecta
Giant Window Pane Palm
Solitary palm, eventually tall but ideal for growing in a tub when young. Large, matt-green leaves have notches at their tips. Position in partial to heavy shade.
USA Zones 10 and 11

Rhopaloblaste singaporensis
Kerinting
This clump-forming palm's leaves are formed of many stiff, spreading, narrow, mid-green leaflets. Position in a shady, wind-sheltered spot.
USA Zones 10 and 11

Siphokentia beguinii
Solitary, slender palm with shiny green leaves divided into both broad and narrow leaflets. Needs a partially shaded position and shelter from strong wind.
USA Zones 10 and 11

A-Z Groundcovering palms

Many palms have stems above and below the ground's surface that help to create groundcover rather than a single upright plant. Here are a few of them.

Other groundcovering palms

Brahea decumbens
Small, slow-growing palm with a spreading nature; produces offsets and seedlings that help it spread. Has a crowded nature and develops attractive, bluish-green, fan-shaped leaves. In the wild it appears near indestructible and grows well in poor, well-drained soil in full sun. USA Zones 8 to 11

Chamaedorea brachypoda
Clustering and clump-forming palm that forms crowded groups. It grows rapidly in its native Central America and in rich, moisture-retentive soil and full sun; elsewhere, growth is much slower. Slender stems bear dark-green leaves, slightly notched at the tips. USA Zones 10b and 11

Licuala sarawakensis
Dwarf, clump-forming palm, seldom more than 1m (3½ft) high, with short stems and dark-green leaves formed of 6–7 wedge-shaped segments. Needs a tropical environment and light shade. USA Zones 10b and 11

Pinanga disticha
Dwarf, spreading palm with a suckering and clump-forming nature. Spreads rapidly when given moderately moist, fertile soil, light shade and warmth. Dark-green, attractively marbled leaves are notched at their ends. USA Zones 10b and 11

Pinanga pilosa
Small, clump-forming palm with slender stems and arching, feather-like, light- to medium-green leaves with dark-green to brown mottling. Keep soil moist and position in light shade. USA Zones 10 and 11

Reinhardtia simplex
Small, clustering palm, rarely more than 1.2m (4ft) high, with glossy, deep-green leaves, light green beneath. Sometimes they are undivided, or divided into 3 leaflets. Needs a warm, tropical climate and light shade. USA Zones 10b and 11

Sabal etonia
Scrub Palmetto
This robust palm has underground stems and light-green to yellowish-green leaves, 60cm (2ft) wide, with threads hanging from parts of the divisions. Tolerant of drought, grows well in shade or full sun and thrives in light, sandy soil. USA Zones 8 to 11

A-Z Hedge and screening palms

Other hedging and screening palms

Aiphanes eggersii
Clumping palm with slender stems that grow to 4.5m (15ft) or more high. Green leaves with wedge-shaped segments; the undersides of the leaves are whitish.
USA Zones 10b and 11

Aiphanes macroloba
Clumping, clustering palm with a radically informal nature and slender stems 2.1m (7ft) or more high, bearing graceful fronds formed of about 8 large, green segments. Grows naturally in light shade, with shelter from strong wind that may split the leaves. Not widely available, but deserves greater recognition.
USA Zones 10b and 11

Areca macrocarpa
Clustering, clump-forming palm with stout stems reaching 4.5m (15ft) or more high, with crowns of overlapping, dark-green leaves. Warmth and light shade are essential for rapid growth, as are fertile, moisture-retentive soil throughout the year.
USA Zones 10b and 11

Arenga tremula
Clustering, clump-forming palm with slender trunks up to 3.6m (12ft) high and a spreading crown bearing dark-green leaves, dull and glaucous beneath. Succeeds in light shade or full sun, with moisture-retentive but well-drained soil.
USA Zones 10 and 11

Bactris major
Clustering palm with slender stems 9m (30ft) or more high, bearing clusters of dull-green fronds, 2.4m (8ft) long. Mature specimens sometimes have a spread of 7.5m (25ft) or more, and form dramatic screens. Grows well in full sun once established, but needs light shade when young.
USA Zones 10 and 11

Calyptrocalyx hollrungii
Clustering palm often forming large, dense clumps. Leaf shape is variable, some revealing finely divided and narrow green segments, while others are broad. Young leaves are frequently wine-coloured. Needs a warm, tropical area, with light shade.
USA Zones 10a and 11

Chamaedorea costaricana
Costa Rican Bamboo Palm
Graceful, clumping palm that grows to 3.6–6m (12–20ft) high, sometimes more, and forms a clump up to 3m (10ft) wide. Olive-green to dull deep-green leaves, 1.2m (4ft) long, are borne on arching leafstalks and form a dramatic feature. Needs a warm environment, moisture-retentive but well-drained soil and light shade, especially when young.
USA Zones 10 and 11

Chuniophoenix nana
Forms compact clumps with many slender stems bearing circular, glossy, mid-green leaves formed of about 6 segments. Grows up to 1.2m (4ft) high and is a warmth-loving palm, for tropical and sub-tropical regions. Fertile, moisture-retentive soil and light shade ensures rapid growth; avoid full and strong sunlight.
USA Zones 10 and 11

Cyrtostachys glauca
Clustering, clump-forming palm, sometimes with 1–2 tall stems, up to 9m (30ft) high, but mainly with clustering sucker-like shoots that are much lower. Bears spreading, drooping, bright-green leaves up to 3m (10ft) long. Needs tropical or subtropical conditions and fertile, well-drained but moisture-retentive soil. Grows best in good light. Shelter from strong wind, especially when young.
USA Zones 10 and 11

Nypa fruticans
Nipah, Mangrove Palm
Clustering though solitary-trunked palm. Essentially a fast-growing tropical type that especially enjoys moisture and is used to stabilize soil at the edges of ponds, streams and rivers. Grows best in full sun and is not suitable for coastal areas, where the water is saline. Has a large and dramatic nature, with light-green or yellowish-green leaves.
USA Zones 10b and 11

Pinanga densiflora
Clumping, densely clustering palm, 2.1–3m (7–10ft) or more high. It is packed with light-green leaves that reveal pinkish hues and chocolate-brown blotches. With age, leaves become bluish-green to deep green, sometimes with dark-green blotches. Fertile, moisture-retentive soil and tropical warmth are essential. Grows best in semi-shade, but will grow in full sun once established.
USA Zones 10b and 11

Ptychosperma lauterbachii
With both a solitary and clustering nature, this palm creates a magnificent screen of matte-green, narrow to wedge-shaped leaves, 2.7m (9ft) long. Tropical warmth is essential, as well as moisture-retentive soil that does not dry out. Grows in semi-shade or full sun.
USA Zones 10b and 11

Raphia vinifera
African Bamboo Palm
Distinctive tropical palm with tall, bamboo-like stems, 4.5m (15ft) or more high. Sucker-like growths develop from its base and form clumps packed with shiny, dark-green, feather-like leaves with long leaflets. Undersides of leaves are glaucous and waxy. Needs warmth and moisture-retentive soil that does not dry out. Grows in full sun, even when young.
USA Zones 10b and 11

Syagrus vagans
Clustering palm with leaves growing directly from the ground and reaching about 1.8m (6ft) high. Stems are stiffly erect, formed of deep-green leaflets. The underground stems are apt to spread. Grows best in full sun and well-drained soil.
USA Zones 10 and 11

A-Z Palms for dry and relatively dry soils

To various degrees, some palms can survive in dry soils, although this may not encourage the best or healthiest growth. Once established and growing strongly, many palms can tolerate dry soil.

Washingtonia, Mexican Fan Palm, Skyduster, Southern Washingtonia, Thread Palm

Other palms for relatively dry soils once established

Phoenix theophrasti
Cretan Date Palm

It can survive relatively dry soil once established. Resembles *Phoenix dactylifera*, with a clustering and small stature. The leafy crown is formed of leaves with grey-green to bluish grey-green leaflets. Grows in full sun and fertile, moisture-retentive soil.
USA Zones 8 to 11

Sabal mauritiiformis
Bay Leaf Palm

A dominant palm growing 18m (60ft) or more high. Can withstand slight dryness in the soil once established, and grows best in medium to full sun. The slender, grey-brown trunk bears green, palmate leaves. Best suited to tropical and subtropical regions.
USA Zones 10 and 11

Sabal mexicana
Texas Palmetto, Rio Grande Palmetto, Texas Sabal

Has a robust nature, with a grey trunk about 15m (50ft) high and a crown of thread-bearing, dark-green leaves. Grows best in medium to full sun. Once established, it can survive relatively dry soil.
USA Zones 9 and 10

Other palms for dry soils

Brahea dulcis Rock Palm
Naturally grows in poor, rocky soil and can thus survive dryness in the soil. It needs full sun. Robust palm, with a trunk up to 6m (20ft) high and 25cm (10in) in diameter. The leafy crown has yellowish-green or bluish-green leaves.
USA Zones 9 to 11

Butia yatay Yatay Palm
Attractive palm, often grown in light, sandy, well-drained soil and therefore well able to thrive in moderately dry areas. Grows up to 12m (40ft) high, with attractive bluish fronds. Thrives in direct sunlight.
USA Zones 9 to 11

Copernicia alba Caranday Palm
Fast-growing South American palm with a slender trunk, 25m (80ft) or more high, and a crown of leaves with greyish-green segments, 90cm (3ft) wide. Requires full sun and survives in slightly dry soil.
USA Zones 9b to 11

Copernicia baileyana Bailey Fan Palm
Trunk is about 12m (40ft) high, with a rounded crown packed with nearly circular light- to deep-green leaf segments, 1.5m (5ft) wide. Tolerates slightly dry soil, but grows faster in moist conditions in full sun.
USA Zones 10 and 11

Copernicia berteroana
Often planted in groups or 3–5 as an ornamental landscape feature in warm climates. Has a trunk about 9m (30ft) high and a crown of grassy-green leaves, 90cm (3ft) wide. Tolerates dry soil, but grows faster in moist conditions in full sun.
USA Zones 10 and 11

Copernicia fallaensis
Majestic palm that needs to be more widely grown, especially in a group and as an ornamental feature. It develops a trunk 9m (30ft) or more high, topped with a large crown of rounded to diamond-shaped leaves, 2.4m (8ft) wide, with silvery blue-green segments. Tolerant of dry soil, but grows faster in moist conditions in full sun.
USA Zones 10 and 11

Copernicia rigida
Distinctive slow-growing palm, especially while young, when it bears a slight resemblance to a yucca. Eventually grows 7.5m (25ft) or more high, with erect, medium-green, narrow leaves. Tolerates dry soil, but needs full sun.
USA Zones 10 and 11

Dypsis decaryi Triangle Palm
Beautiful, solitary-trunked, ornamental palm for landscape planting, with a trunk 7.5m (25ft) or more high and revealing a crown of 3m (10ft) long leaves packed with greyish-green to bluish-green leaflets. Survives in considerably dry soil, but grows better in moisture-retentive soil and full sun.
USA Zones 10 and 11

Livistona decipiens Fountain Palm, Ribbon Palm
Has a solitary trunk and leafy crown packed with up to 60 leaves, each 2.7m (9ft) wide. Leaflets are bluish-green. Tolerant of dry soil, but grows better in moisture-retentive soil with full sun.
USA Zones 9 to 11

Livistona inermis Wispy Fan Palm
Has a slender, solitary trunk, 7.5m (25ft) or more high, and a branching, clustered head formed of nearly circular light-green to greyish-green leaves, 60cm (2ft) wide. Has a slow-growing nature and survives in well-drained soil and full sun.
USA Zones 10 and 11

Livistona mariae Central Australian Cabbage Palm
One of the palm-world's survivors, it is slow growing, with a solitary trunk up to 25m (80ft) high and leaves 1.8m (6ft) long, sparsely clothed in greyish-green segments.

Tolerates drought, but grows faster with adequate moisture. Grows best in full sun, even when young.
USA Zones 10 and 11

Livistona rotundifolia Footstool Palm, Serdang
Has a solitary trunk up to 25m (80ft) high, and glossy, round, deep-green leaves about 1.5m (5ft) wide. Requires a hot climate and full sun, but survives light shade when young. Tolerates dry soil but grows best when given adequate water and fertile soil.
USA Zones 10b and 11

Syagrus coronata Ouricury Palm, Licury Palm
This distinctive palm has a solitary trunk covered by old leaf-bases. It grows 9m (30ft) or more high, with bluish-green, graceful, arching leaves. Survives in dry soil but needs a warm climate and full sun.
USA Zones 10 nd 11

Syagrus glaucescens
Has a solitary trunk about 3m (10ft) high, and leaves 90cm (3ft) wide, formed of bluish or silvery-grey leaflets. Thrives in well-drained soil and full sun.
USA Zones 10 and 11

Syagrus vagans
Clustering palm, about 2.1m (7ft) high, with stiffly erect stems that grow directly from the ground and produce a large tuft of glaucous, deep-green leaflets. Grows in freely draining soil and full sun.
USA Zones 10a and 11

Trithrinax brasiliensis
Has either a clumping nature or a solitary trunk, with green to greyish green leaves, 90cm–1.2m (3–4ft) wide, formed of stiff, spreading segments. The solitary trunks are usually 7.5–9m (25–30ft) high, but taller in the wild. Tolerant of dry soil, but grows faster when given adequate moisture and full sun.
USA Zones 9 to 11

Palms for wet, swampy soils

Most palms grow best when given a moderate amount of moisture in the soil, but some can grow in exceptionally moist soil, even swampy conditions.

SPECIES	PAGE

Acoelorraphe wrightii   **45**
Everglades Palm, Paurotis Palm, Saw Cabbage Palm, Silver Saw Palm, Silver Saw Palmetto

Copernicia macroglossa   **80**
Cuban Petticoat Palm, Jata de Guanbacoa, Petticoat Palm

Cyrtostachys renda   **82**
Lipstick Palm, Maharajah Palm, Pinang-rajah, Rajah Palm, Sealing Wax Palm

Elaeis guineensis   **86**
African Oil Palm, Macaw Fat, Oil Palm

Euterpe edulis   **87**
Assai Palm, Jacara Palm

Hydriastele wendlandiana   **91**
Florence Falls Palm, Latrum Palm

Livistona australis   **103**
Australian Cabbage Palm, Australian Palm, Australian Fan Palm, Cabbage Palm, Fan Palm, Gippsland Palm

Metroxylon sagu   **107**
Sago Palm

Phoenix roebelenii   **115**
Dwarf Date Palm, Miniature Date Palm, Pygmy Date Palm, Roebelin Palm

Ptychosperma macarthurii   **122**
Hurricane Palm, Macarthur Feather Palm, Macarthur Palm

Raphia farinifera   **123**
Madagascar Raffia Palm, Raffia Palm

Ravenea rivularis   **124**
Majesty Palm

Rhapidophyllum hystrix   **126**
Blue Palmetto, Creeping Palmetto, Dwarf Saw Palmetto, Hedgehog Palm, Needle Palm, Porcupine Palm, Spine Palm, Vegetable Porcupine

Roystonea regia   **130**
Cuban Royal, Cuban Royal Palm, Florida Royal Palm, Royal Palm

Other palms for wet, swampy soils

Areca whitfordii
Solitary-trunked palm, about 6m (20ft) high, sometimes slightly more, with arching fronds packed with deep-green leaves formed of 90cm (3ft) leaflets. This tropical palm grows in semi-swampy areas in its native Philippines. Grows well in full sun.
USA Zones 10b and 11.

Arenga microcarpa   Lang Kap
Known as the Aren Sagu, this clump-forming, suckering palm grows about 7.5m (25ft) high, with thin stems and spreading glossy dark-green leaves with silvery under-sides. Needs tropical conditions, full sun and continually wet soil, perhaps near a stream.
USA Zones 10b and 11.

Arenga obtusifolia
Vigorous, clump-forming palm with trunks often 15m (50ft) high. The crowded, dark-green leaflets, silver below, form leaves 5.4m (18ft) long. Warmth, full sun and constant soil moisture are essential, as are rich and fertile conditions.
USA Zones 10b and 11.

Dypsis rivularis
With a solitary trunk and stilt roots, it grows 3.6m (12ft) or slightly higher, with gracefully arching, medium- to dark-green leaves. Needs a warm climate, light shade and moisture-retentive soil that does not dry out.
USA Zones 10b and 11.

Elaeis oleifera   American Oil Palm
This native of tropical America has leaves formed of deep-green leaflets, 60cm (2ft) long. The older part of the trunk has a prostrate nature, the young part is upright. The trunk's ground-hugging nature encourages it to produce aerial roots. It is a warmth-loving palm for light shade or full sun, with its roots in constantly wet soil.
USA Zones 10b and 11

Gulubia costata
Tall palm with a solitary trunk, 30m (100ft) high, and leaves up to 4.5m (15ft) long, formed of dark-green leaflets 90cm–1.2m (3–4ft) long and about 5cm (2in) wide. Its tropical nature needs full sun and plenty of moisture in the soil.
USA Zones 10b and 11

Licuala ramsayi   Australian Fan Palm
Has a solitary trunk, usually about 12m (40ft) high, and leaves, 1.5m (5ft) long, formed of mid-green, wedge-shaped segments. This warmth-loving palm thrives in full sun, with roots in constantly moist, fertile soil.
USA Zones 10b and 11

Palms for small gardens

Sabal minor

Palms for coastal gardens

Saline conditions in the soil and air are a challenge in coastal gardens. Here are a few palms to consider.s

Phoenix dactylifera

A-Z

Cycads for warm regions

Other cycads for warm regions
SUBTROPICAL TO TROPICAL REGIONS

Bowenia spectabilis Zamia Fern
Has subterranean stems and glossy, dark-green leaves, bright green when young. Initially stems are upright, then spreading. Female cones are egg-shaped to globular, about 10cm (4in) long and 10cm (4in) wide; male cones are somewhat cylindrical, about 7.5cm (3in) long and up to 25mm (1in) wide. It is native to Queensland, Australia, and needs a warm position. Grows in full sun, light or deep shade.

Ceratozamia miqueliana
Has subterranean stems and arching, glaucous-green leaves, 1.2–1.8m (4–6ft) long and about 60cm (2ft) wide. Female cones are cylindrical and upright, about 15cm (6in) long and up to 10cm (4in) wide; male cones are conical, 20–25cm (8–10in) long and about 36mm (1½in) wide. It is native to Mexico and needs warmth and light shade.

Cycas litoralis
Has an arborescent nature, growing 3–9m (10–30ft) high, with spreading, glossy, bright-green leaves up to 2.4m (8ft) long and 60cm (2ft) wide. Female cones have an open nature, with sporophylls 30–50cm (12–20in) long; male cones are oval, up to 40cm (16in) long and about 12cm (4½in) wide. Native to the shorelines of Vietnam, Thailand, Malaysia and Sumatra. Grows in light shade to full sun and thrives in well-drained soil.

Encephalartos laurentianus
Perhaps the largest cycad, initially upright and later spreading to 15m (50ft) or more. The erect, then spreading, leaves are formed of about 120 pairs of greyish leaflets. Female cones are somewhat oblong to oval, up to 45cm (18in) long and about 20cm (8in) wide; male cones are somewhat conical, about 35cm (14in) long and 10cm (4in) wide. Native to Tropical Africa. Grows in full sun and moisture-retentive, moderately fertile soil.

Microcycas calocoma Cork Palm, Palma Corcho
This large cycad has a tree-like nature and a trunk up to 9m (30ft) high, sometimes more, and 60cm (2ft) in diameter; sometimes it is branched as a result of damage. The straight, dark-green leaves are 60cm–1m (2–3½ft) long and 18–25cm (7–10in) wide. Each has 50–80 pairs of leaflets, up to 18cm (7in) long and about 12mm (½in) wide. In arid conditions it becomes deciduous or

semi-deciduous, but remains evergreen when given fertile, moisture-retentive soil. It is sensitive to frost.

Zamia encephalartoides
Sometimes with a recumbent nature, this cycad produces stems about 1.8m (6ft) long and slightly arching leaves up to 1m (3½ft) long, with up to 40 pairs of dark-green leaflets, 20–30cm (8–12in) long and 30mm (1¼in) wide. Female cones are oval to cylindrical, about 38cm (15in) long and 10–15cm (4–6in) wide; male cones are cylindrical, 20–30cm (8–12in) long and about 5cm (2in) wide. Native to Colombia. Best suited to full sun and well-drained soil.

Zamia tuerckheimii
Young stems tend to be subterranean, while older ones are arborescent and up to 3m (10ft) long, with arching, glossy-green leaves up to 1.8m (6ft) long. Female cones are usually cylindrical, 18cm (7in) long and about 7.5cm (3in) wide; male cones are narrowly cylindrical, about 18cm (7in) long and 25mm (1in) wide. Mainly native to Guatemala. Grows in light shade and moisture-retentive soil.

Other cycads for warm regions
WARM TO WARM-TEMPERATE REGIONS

Bowenia serrulata Byfield Fern
Subterranean stems and erect, glossy, dark-green leaves to 1.8m (6ft) high. Female cones, upright and somewhat spherical, are 10cm (4in) long and 13cm (5in) wide; male cones are nearly cylindrical, 7.5–10cm (3–4in) long and 42mm (1¾in) wide. Native to coastal Queensland, Australia. Grows best in light shade and moisture-retentive but well-drained, fertile soil.

Cycas desolata
It develops upright stems to about 4m (13ft), with glaucous-blue leaves 1m (3½ft) long and bearing up to 68 pairs of leaflets. Female cones are

open types (where the sporophylls are long and lax); male cones are somewhat oval, up to 40cm (16in) long and 8cm (3¼in) wide. Native to Queensland, Australia. Full sun and well-drained soil suit it.

Cycas hainanensis
Erect, arborescent stems, up to 3.6m (12ft) high, with glossy, dark-green, spreading leaves about 3m (10ft) long and nearly 60cm (2ft) wide. They bear up to 45 pairs of narrow leaflets. Female cones have a closed nature and are about 38cm (15in) wide; male cones are somewhat cylindrical, up to 72cm (28in) long and 13cm (5in) wide.

Native to China. Grows in light shade and moisture-retentive but well-drained, fertile soil.

Stangeria eriopus Baboon Food
Has subterranean stems and upright or cascading leaves that arise from a crown at ground level and is formed of up to 20 pairs of leaflets. Female cones are somewhat oval, 18cm (7in) long and 8cm (3¼in) wide; male cones are upright and somewhat cylindrical, 10–25cm (4–10in) long and about 36mm (1½in) wide. Native to South Africa. Likes moisture-retentive but well-drained soil and light shade for part of the day.

A–Z
Cycads that tolerate heat and drought

(NOT IN A–Z)

Cycas basaltica
Has arborescent, upright, rarely branched stems to about 3m (10ft) high, and leaves formed of 100 or more pairs of leaflets. Female cones have an open nature; male cones are narrowly oval, up to 35cm (14in) long and 7.5cm (3in) wide. Native to Western Australia. Grows in light shade to full sun and well-drained soil.

Encephalartos cycadifolius
With subterranean stems and a suckering nature it has a clump-forming habit, with leaves up to 90cm (3ft) long and dark, olive-green leaflets. Female cones are barrel-shaped, 20–30cm (8–12in) long and about 18cm (7in) wide; male cones have a cylindrical nature, about 20cm (8in) long and 6.5cm (2½in) wide. Native to South Africa. Needs full sun and well-drained soil.

Encephalartos lanatus
Arborescent stems, usually upright, unbranched and about 1m (3½ft) or slightly more high. The leaves, 60–90cm (2–3ft) long, have leaflets that turn dark green with age. Female cones are barrel-shaped, up to 35cm (14in) long and 15cm (6in) wide; male cones are cylindrical, 25–30cm (10–12in) long and nearly 6cm (2½in) wide. Native to South Africa. Needs full sun and well-drained soil.

Macrozamia macdonnellii
Sometimes upright but often with a leaning and suckering nature, the stems are up to 3m (10ft) long. The leaves, 1.5–2.1m (5–7ft) long, have a spreading and drooping nature, with up to 80 pairs of leaflets. Female cones are oval to cylindrical, up to 50cm (20in) long and 25cm (10in) wide; male cones are cylindrical, 25–40cm (10–16in) long and up to 10cm (4in) wide. Native to Australia. Grows in light shade to full sun and fertile, well-drained soil.

A-Z Cycads that tolerate cold and frost

Cycas couttsiana
Glen Idle Blue

Has upright, seldom branching stems, usually up to 3m (10ft) high, but some reported as 9m (30ft) tall. Leaves are up to 1.3m (4¼ft) long and 38cm (15in) wide; they bear more than 100 pairs of glaucous-blue leaflets. Female cones have an open nature; male cones are oval, 15–20cm (6–8in) long and up to 10cm (4in) wide. Native to Queensland, Australia. Grows in light shade to full sun and well-drained soil.

Cycas megacarpa
Zamia Palm, Pine Palm

Has erect stems, 3m (10ft) or more high, although leaning during its later years. The arching leaves bear 100 or more glossy-green leaflets. Female cones have an open nature; male cones are narrowly oval, about 18cm (7in) long and up to 10cm (4in) wide. Native to Queensland, Australia. Grows in light shade to full sun and well-drained soil.

Dioön tomasellii
It has erect stems, usually about 1m (3½ft) high, and dark-green leaves up to 1.8m (6ft) long and bearing as many as 100 pairs of leaflets. Female cones are oval, 20–30cm (8–12in) long and 15–20cm (6–8in) wide; male cones are cylindrical, up to 50cm (20in) long and 8–10cm (3¼–4in) wide. Native to Mexico. Full sun or light shade and well-drained soil are best.

Encephalartos latifrons
Stems are arborescent, clump-forming and upright to about 3m (10ft) high, with leaves up to 1.5m (5ft) long and bearing broad leaflets. Female cones are large and barrel-shaped, about 60cm (2ft) long and 25cm (10in) wide, whereas male cones are somewhat cylindrical, 30–50cm (12–20in) long and up to 15cm (6in) wide. Native to South Africa. Needs full sun and well-drained soil.

A-Z Cycads for full sun

A-Z Cycads for wet soil

A-Z Cycads that tolerate full shade

5

A–Z
of
palms

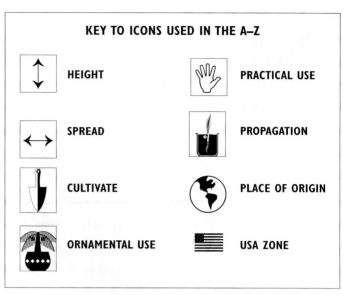

KEY TO ICONS USED IN THE A–Z

↕	HEIGHT	✋	PRACTICAL USE
↔	SPREAD		PROPAGATION
🔨	CULTIVATE	🌍	PLACE OF ORIGIN
🌴	ORNAMENTAL USE	🇺🇸	USA ZONE

This A–Z of palms covers 100 species, revealing their natures and variations in growth, from those with trunks to those with a clump-forming or scrambling habit. In addition to these, many others are featured in Chapter 4; they encompass palms as houseplants and in conservatories, in tubs outdoors, as groundcovering plants, as hedges and screens, and also highlight those that like dry or wet soils.

In this chapter, indications of the height and spread are suggested for each palm, but this varies according to the plant's growth and maturity. In their native areas most palms grow taller than when planted in gardens or used as ornamental features. One exception is *Chamaerops humilis*, the European Fan Palm, which tends to grow taller in cultivation than in the wild. This is because it forms clumps in the wild, but often has a solitary trunk in cultivation.

Many palms can also be grown indoors or in conservatories (see pages 31–32) or as features in tubs outdoors in warm countries (see pages 33–34). In these cases, the height is less than when planted in the ground outdoors, especially when indoors in temperate climates.

Names in brackets are those used earlier for that palm; they may still be seen in earlier books and in some palm catalogues. Note that where common names are not given, they do not appear to exist.

Acoelorraphe wrightii

(Acoelorraphe arborescens, Paurotis wrightii, Paurotis androsana, Acanthosabal caespitosa)

Everglades Palm, Paurotis Palm, Saw Cabbage Palm, Silver Saw Palm, Silver Saw Palmetto

This moderately fast-growing palm has fan-shaped, bright-green leaves, silver beneath, 60–90cm (2–3ft) across and borne on 90cm (3ft) leafstalks. Each leaf is deeply divided to about halfway and formed of many tapering segments. Flower stalks appear from among the leaves, with tightly packed, small white flowers. Small, round fruits ripen to shiny black. This clump-forming palm has a suckering nature, with stems up to 10cm (4in) wide.

FACT FILE

 4.5–6m (15–20ft), but sometimes to 10.5m (35ft) or more

 4.5m (15ft) or more across

 It thrives in moist soil and full sun, but tolerates slight shade and moderately dry soil. It grows well in coastal areas and is fundamentally a palm for the tropics or subtropics. Once established, however, it is hardy and grows well in warm-temperate climates. Fertile, neutral to slightly acidic soil is essential.

 Clothed in attractive leaves down to ground level, it is ideal for planting in a large border or as a specimen palm in a lawn. It is superb for creating a hedge or screen in tropical and subtropical regions. It is not suitable as an indoor palm in temperate climates, although it is frequently planted as a tub plant on a patio or in a courtyard in tropical and subtropical regions.

 Sow fresh seed, which is small and germinates within 12 weeks. However, it is easier to increase this palm by removing established suckers and transfering them to pots of compost.

 Wide area, including West Indies, southern Florida, Mexico and Central America; mainly in moisture-retentive and swampy ground

 USA Zone 9b to 11

A-Z PALMS

Adonidia merrillii

 15m (50ft) in the wild, less in cultivation and usually 4.5–6m (15–20ft)

 3.6–4.5m (12–15ft)

 Plant in moisture-retentive but well-drained soil in light shade or full sun. A tropical or subtropical region is essential for this palm, which grows rapidly when young. It grows well in coastal areas.

 It is ideal for planting in an ornamental lawn in tropical or subtropical areas, preferably in a group of three. It is sometimes used for indoor decoration.

 Sow fresh seed, which germinates within 12 weeks.

 Philippines USA Zones 10b and 11

(Veitchia merrillii)
Adonidia Palm, Christmas Palm, Dwarf Royal Palm, Manila Palm

Green leaflets with pendent ends are borne in a V-shaped formation on arching leaves, 1.8–2.4m (6–8ft) long, with 30cm (12in) leafstalks. Each palm has about 12 leaves. White flowers are followed by grape-like fruits that mature to bright red or scarlet. The solitary, light- to dark-grey trunk is 25–30cm (10–12in) in diameter.

Aiphanes aculeata

(Aiphanes caryotifolia, Aiphanes elegans,
Aiphanes orinocensis, Martinezia caryotifolia)
Chonta Ruro, Coyure Palm, Ruffle Palm, Spine Palm

Deep glossy-green leaflets, pale green beneath, form leaves 1.5–2.4m (5–8ft) long, each with 50–80 leaflets. This fast-growing palm has 10–15 leaves. The irregular-shaped leaflets grow at different angles from the leaf stems to produce an attractive, ruffled nature. Yellowish-white flowers are followed by fruits, 25mm (1in) wide, that mature to orange or red. The solitary trunk, ringed in black spines, is about 15cm (6in) in diameter.

FACT FILE

 7.5–10.5m (25–35ft) in the wild, less in cultivation

 3–5.4m (10–18ft)

 Fertile, moisture-retentive but well-drained soil in light shade, especially when in tropical regions with high light intensity.

 Suitable for planting as a specimen palm in tropical and subtropical regions, or in a container in a conservatory in warm-temperate climates. As a houseplant, it needs light shade. It also grows well as a tub plant outdoors in tropical and sub-tropical regions. For safety reasons, remove the spines from the trunks of palms that are grown ornamentally.

 Sow fresh seed, which germinates in 12–15 weeks.

 Venezuela, Colombia, Bolivia, Peru (mainly along the Andes)

 USA Zones 10b and 11

Aiphanes erosa

 4.5–6m (15–20ft); claims are made of heights up to 15m (50ft), but in cultivation 4.5m (15ft) is more realistic

 3.6–4.5m (12–15ft)

 Fertile, well-drained but moisture-retentive soil in partial shade or full sun. It is only suitable for warm climates.

 Suitable for planting as a specimen palm in tropical or subtropical regions. If planted in a group, ensure the foliage does not encroach on neighbouring palms as its distinctive nature will be spoiled. For safety reasons, remove the spines from the trunks of palms that are grown ornamentally.

 The fleshy fruits were formerly eaten by local peoples.

 Sow fresh seed, which germinates in 12–15 weeks.

 West Indies

 USA Zone 10b

(Aiphanes minima, Martinezia erosa)
Macaw Palm

Dark, bright-green leaflets, pale green beneath and up to 25cm (10in) long, form leaves 1.8–2.4m (6–8ft) long. This palm is clad in spines from an early age, but has a less ruffled appearance than *Aiphanes aculeata*, with leaflets regularly spaced and angled along the leaf stem. Fragrant, yellowish flowers are followed by edible 12mm (½in) fruits that ripen to red. This slim, moderately fast-growing palm has a solitary trunk covered in sharp, black spines.

Archontophoenix alexandrae

Alex Palm, Alexandra King Palm, Alexandra Palm,
King Palm, Northern Bangalow Palm

Bright- to deep-green, grey or silvery beneath, strongly ribbed and narrow leaflets are attached to central stems, 1.8–3m (6–10ft) long. These are sometimes slightly twisted, so the stiff leaflets are upright, facing downward or to the sides. The flowers are white or cream, with small, round fruits that are red when mature. In cultivation, the light-grey to olive-green trunk is 23–30cm (9–12in) in diameter, prominently ringed and with a bulge at its base.

FACT FILE

 18–25m (60–80ft) in the wild, but usually 6–9m (20–30ft) in cultivation

 The head in older palms is up to 6m (20ft) across

 Claimed to be the fastest growing of all cultivated palms. Moisture-retentive and fertile soil suits it best; if the soil does not retain sufficient water, the leaves are usually damaged during dry periods. It is said to withstand temperatures a few degrees below freezing, but will be severely damaged if this is combined with frozen water around the roots. It likes high temperatures, good light and relatively high humidity.

 Young plants are often planted in large tubs outdoors in tropical and subtropical regions. Always buy container-grown specimens for planting into a garden; this helps reduce root disturbance when it is planted. When young, it is also suited to large conservatories. As a houseplant it needs good light. It is a superb landscape palm for large gardens, and is used as a street tree.

 Sow fresh seed, which germinates in 6–12 weeks.

 Mainly northern and coastal Queensland, Australia

 USA Zones 10b and 11

A–Z PALMS

Archontophoenix cunninghamiana

FACT FILE

15–21m (50–70ft) in the wild, but usually 6–7.5m (20–25ft) in cultivation

The head on older palms is up to 4.5m (15ft) wide

Fast-growing palm that likes moisture-retentive fertile soil; if the soil does not retain sufficient water, the leaves are often damaged during dry periods. It is slightly less tender than *Archontophoenix alexandrae* and thrives in warm-temperate areas, as well as tropical and subtropical regions. It likes high temperatures, good light and relatively high humidity.

Young plants are often planted in large tubs outdoors in tropical and subtropical regions. Always buy container-grown specimens for planting into a garden; this helps reduce root disturbance when it is planted. When young, it is suited to large conservatories. As a houseplant it needs good light.

Sow fresh seed, which germinates in 6–12 weeks.

Mainly the coastal area of Queensland and into the eastern parts of New South Wales, Australia

USA Zone 10a

Bangalow Palm, Piccabeen Bangalow Palm, Piccabeen Palm

Mid- to dark-green, narrow leaflets that tend to droop from the arching leaves, which are 2.4–3m (8–10ft) long. The 90cm (3ft) leaflets are coppery or bronze when young, with green undersides. The palm has lavender flowers and pink to red fruits. The trunk is up to 25cm (10in) in diameter; unlike *Archontophoenix alexandrae*, it is only slightly swollen at its base, but with deep rings.

Areca catechu

Areca Nut Palm, Betel Nut Palm, Betel Palm, Caccu, Catechu, Pinang

The shiny green leaves are about 2.4m (8ft) long and arching, each bearing 40 or more jagged ended leaflets. The greyish-green trunk has whitish rings. Fragrant whitish-yellow flowers are followed by egg-shaped, yellow fruits, 2.5–5cm (1–2in) long, which ripen to red. The trunk is usually about 20cm (8in) wide.

FACT FILE

 9–15m (30–50ft) in the wild, although often claimed to grow to 30m (100ft); it is usually seen no higher than 7.5m (25ft)

 The head in older palms is usually about 3.6m (12ft) wide

 It is fast growing and needs moisture-retentive but well-drained, fertile, slightly acid soil and full sun or partial shade. It requires a warm temperature, in the tropics or subtropics.

 Although mainly grown commercially, it is sometimes planted in groups as an ornamental feature. It is ideal for creating groundcover in the tropics and subtropics.

 Mainly grown commercially for use in betel, which is chewed as a mild narcotic across south and east Asia.

 Thought to have originated in the Malay Peninsula, but now widely naturalized and cultivated in southeast Malaysia, Indonesia, the Philippines, South Pacific Islands, India and Sri Lanka

 USA Zones 10b and 11

A–Z PALMS

Arenga caudata

FACT FILE

1.8–2.1m (6–7ft)

Clumps are often 1.8m (6ft) across, or more

Requires fertile, moisture-retentive but well-drained soil and, in cold areas, shelter from strong wind, growing best in lightly filtered sunlight or full sun. It flourishes in tropical and subtropical regions, as well as warm-temperate areas.

In warm areas it is sometimes used to form a hedge or screen. It is also used as a landscape feature where a dominant and hedge-like display is needed. In tropical, subtropical and warm-temperate climates it is used as an outdoor tub plant: position the container in full sun or light shade. As a houseplant it needs full sun or slight shade. Beware of touching the seeds and fruit, which are caustic.

It is not easily increased, either by seed or division. Seed is both slow and reluctant to germinate; soaking seeds in water for 5–6 days before sowing increases the chances of germination. Suckers removed from a parent plant are slow to become established.

Thailand, Malaysia, Cambodia, Vietnam and southern China

USA Zones 9b to 11

(Didymosperma caudata)
Dwarf Sugar Palm

Densely clump-forming, slow-growing small palm with leaves about 90cm (3ft) long, borne on 45cm (18in) leafstalks. Each bears 4–10 wedge-shaped, glossy-green leaflets, silvery-white beneath. The terminal leaflet of each leaf has a distinctive jagged end, while the contrasting colours of the leaf surfaces are revealed when they are rustled by light winds. It bears fragrant, creamy-white flowers, followed by small, egg-shaped, brilliant red fruits.

Arenga engleri

Dwarf Sugar Palm, Sugar Palm, Formosa Palm

This handsome, relatively low-growing palm has green, narrow leaflets, silvery beneath. They are up to 60cm (2ft) long and borne on leaves 2.7m (9ft) long, which have an attractive twisting nature. Fragrant orange and yellow flowers are followed by small, purplish fruits. The palm grows moderately fast when given ideal conditions.

FACT FILE

3–4.5m (10–15ft), but usually less and with several trunks

Forms a clump 3–4.5m (10–15ft) wide

It is best in full sun, but also grows well in partial shade. Moisture-retentive soil encourages rapid growth. It is one of the hardiest palms in this genus and grows best in tropical and subtropical regions; also survives in warm-temperate climates.

Frequently grown as an ornamental palm and, because it is clothed in leaves nearly to its base, is often planted in large lawns. (Note that seeds and fruit are caustic.) Also used to form a large screen or informal hedge, or grown in large containers in conservatories, where it needs good light. It grows outdoors in tubs in subtropical and warm-temperate areas: position the container in full sun. It tolerates a few degrees of frost.

Not easily increased by seed or division. Seed is both slow and reluctant to germinate; soaking seeds in water for 5–6 days before sowing increases the chances of germination. Suckers removed from a parent plant are slow to become established.

The Ryukyu Islands and Taiwan (earlier known as Formosa, from where it gains one of its common names)

USA Zones 9b to 11

A–Z PALMS

Arenga pinnata

 12–18m (40–60ft) in the wild, less in cultivation

 The head in older palms is 6–7.5m (20–25ft) across, sometimes more

 Fertile, well-drained but moisture-retentive soil in slight shade or full sun suits it. It can also survive in slightly dry soil.

 Often grown in small groups in large areas, where it is not constricted by other palms.

 Seed may be slow and reluctant to germinate (though some palm experts claim germination is easy and fast). Soaking seeds in water for 5–6 days before sowing increases the chances of fast germination.

 This palm is well known for its sap, which is extracted and evaporated to produce palm sugar, while the fermented juice becomes palm wine or toddy, which on distillation yields the spirit, arrack. The pith is used as a source of starch, a minor source of sago, while the leaves provide fibre and trunks are used as water pipes.

 Thought to be the Malay Peninsula and western Indonesia

 USA Zone 10b

(Arenga saccharifera)

Aren, Areng Palm, Black Fibre Palm, Gomuti Palm, Kabong, Sugar Palm

This fast-growing palm has stiffly erect leaves, up to 9m (30ft) long, with 90cm (3ft) leaflets that are dark green above and silvery beneath. They are borne at irregular angles, creating a spectacular sight. As the palm reaches maturity it develops branched stems, up to 2.1m (7ft) long, that bear purplish flowers with an unusual aroma. These are followed by clusters of greenish-yellow, oblong fruits. Do not touch the flesh of the fruit as it is poisonous to unprotected hands. Compared to many palms, it has a relatively short life, reaching maturity at 10–15 years and dying within a few years of flowering and bearing fruits. The solitary trunk, 30cm (12in) or more in diameter, assumes a dramatic and complex nature when clothed in spines, old leaf bases and black fibres.

Arenga undulatifolia

(Arenga ambong)
Aren Gelora

Dark-green leaflets, silvery-green to white beneath, are about 90cm (3ft) long, with wavy edges and borne on leaves up to 3m (10ft) long. Flower stalks bear greenish-white flowers, followed by round, purplish-red to brown fruits, 25mm (1in) wide. Trunks are usually solitary and each about 20cm (8in) in diameter, though it is sometimes densely clustered and clump-forming, with several stems.

FACT FILE

 6–9m (20–30ft) in the wild

 Clump forming, to about 6m (20ft) wide

 Moisture-retentive but well-drained fertile soil in full sun suits it best. It forms a dominant display and needs plenty of room to prevent other palms or plants from intruding on its outline. This moderately fast-growing palm does best in tropical and subtropical areas.

 Not easily increased, either by seed or division. Seed is slow and reluctant to germinate; soaking seeds in water for 5–6 days before sowing increases the chances of germination. Some palm experts, however, claim germination is easy and fast. Suckers removed from a parent plant are slow to become established.

 Borneo and Celebes, western Indonesia; the Philippines

 USA Zone 10

Bactris gasipaes

FACT FILE

 12–18m (40–60ft) in the wild, usually less in cultivation

 The head is 4.5–6m (15–20ft) wide in older plants

 Fertile, moisture-retentive but well-drained soil, warmth and full sun encourage rapid growth. Tropical regions produce the best growth, although it also grows in sub-tropical regions.

 Often planted in groups of 3–5 when used as an ornamental feature, and is ideal for creating a hedge or screen in tropical and subtropical regions.

 The peach-like fruits are eaten locally or made into a fermented drink. Oil from the seeds (Oil of Macanilla) is used for cooking. The hard wood is a local building material and sometimes made into bows, while the spines are used for tattooing.

 Sow fresh seed, which germinates within 8–10 weeks. Alternatively, it is possible to divide established plants, but the divisions are usually reluctant to become established.

 Thought to be Central America but now widely cultivated in wet areas of tropical America

 USA Zones 10 and 11

(Bactris speciosa, Bactris utilis, Guilielma speciosa, Guilielma gasipaes)
Chonta, Peach Palm, Pejibaya, Pejibeye, Pejivalle, Pewa, Pupunha

This moderate to fast-growing palm has shiny, deep-green leaflets with a drooping nature and an attractively ringed, spiny trunk, 30cm (12in) or less in diameter. There is a spineless form in cultivation. Leaflets 60–90cm (2–3ft) long are borne on leaves that are 3m (10ft) long, or more. The cream flowers are followed by egg-shaped, edible yellow fruits, 5cm (2in) long, which ripen to red. It has either a solitary or clustering nature.

Bismarckia nobilis

(Medemia nobilis)
Bismarck Palm

Large, waxy, blue-grey or green leaflets are borne on leaves up to 3m (10ft) wide and with a 1.8–2.4m (6–8ft) leafstalk on well-established specimens. Small brown flowers are followed by brown fruits, about 36mm (1½in) wide. The trunk, mainly grey but also tan or brown, is slightly swollen at its base and 30–45cm (12–18in) in diameter. The palm grows quickly when given ideal conditions.

FACT FILE

 18–25m (60–80ft) in the wild, but only half this when cultivated as an ornamental palm

 The head in older palms is 4.5–6m (15–20ft) across

 Well-drained soil and full sun encourage an attractive leaf colour. It can survive dry soil.

 It is widely grown as a specimen palm in the tropics and subtropics.

 Sow fresh seed, which often germinates in 40–60 days, although much longer times have been recorded.

 Madagascar USA Zones 9b to 11

Borassus flabellifer

FACT FILE

 15–18m (50–60ft) in the wild, although occasionally to 30m (100ft); usually 12–15m (40–50ft) when cultivated as a decorative palm

 The head in older palms is about 7.5m (25ft) wide

 Moisture-retentive but essentially well-drained soil is required, although it can survive considerably dry soil. Warmth and full sunlight are vital.

 When planted ornamentally, a large space is needed for this palm to be appreciated from a distance.

 Mature palms provide durable timber for construction. Leaves are used for paper, thatching, and hat- and bag-making, as green manure, and to produce salt and potash. Leaf-base fibres are used for brushes. Female palms bear about 200 nuts annually and their sap makes a refreshing drink. The soft kernel of young fruits is eaten. The inflorescence is tapped for the sugary sap, used to make sugar (jaggery) or fermented for palm wine (toddy) and vinegar.

 The large seeds are usually sown relatively deeply in a large container or directly into the soil. Germination can be fast, but often takes 6 months or more and not all seeds germinate. To help seeds germinate, nick their outsides with a sharp knife or soak in water for a couple of weeks before sowing.

 Claimed to be India, Sri Lanka and Malaysia, but now widely grown in drier areas of Africa, India, Pakistan, Burma, Malaysia and northern Australia

 USA Zones 10 and 11

Doub Palm, Lontar Palm, Palmyra Palm, Panna-maram, Tala Palm, Talauriksha Palm, Tal-gas, Toddy Palm, Wine Palm

Both sides of the leaflets are deep blue-green, and borne on leaves that are 2.4–3m (8–10ft) wide, with 1.8m (6ft) leafstalks. The leaves of young plants often have a bluish tinge. This moderate to fast-growing palm has male and female flowers on separate plants; female flowers are larger than the males and are followed by rounded, shiny, dark-brown fruits up to 20cm (8in) wide and containing three seeds. It is a solitary palm, with a trunk up to 90cm (3ft) in diameter.

Brahea armata

(Brahea roezlii)

Blue Fan Palm, Blue Hesper Palm, Grey Goddess, Mexican Blue Fan Palm, Mexican Blue Palm, Short Blue Hesper

Bluish-green leaves, almost circular and up to 1.8m (6ft) across, are formed of about 50 tapering segments. They are claimed to be at their most attractive in moonlight. Cream flowers are borne in long, arching clusters and followed by fruits, 25mm (1in) wide, which ripen to black. Although it is a slow-growing palm, the solitary trunk is eventually massive – up to 45cm (18in) in diameter, with a slight bulge at its base.

FACT FILE

 12–15m (40–50ft) in the wild, sometimes more

 The head in older palms is 4.5–6m (15–20ft) wide

 Well-drained, slightly alkaline soil, full sun and generous warmth are required. Although it survives a lack of moisture, it grows much better when given sufficient water to encourage steady growth. In cool areas, its roots are at risk if the soil is continually wet.

 In subtropical regions it is often used as a specimen palm in a large lawn. In subtropical and warm-temperate climates it is ideal as a tub plant outdoors: position it in good light. It can tolerate several degrees of frost.

 Sow fresh seed, which usually germinates within 6 months, sometimes 12.

 Baja Peninsula, California; Sonoran Desert, northwest Mexico

 USA Zones 8b to 11

A–Z PALMS

Brahea edulis

 9m (30ft) or more in the wild, less in cultivation

 The head in older palms is usually 3.6m (12ft) across, sometimes slightly more

 This relatively slow-growing palm is best suited to well-drained, poor soil and full sun. A warm climate is essential. It tolerates a few degrees of frost.

 Often grown as a specimen palm in a lawn or as a street tree in subtropical regions.

 Sow fresh seed, which usually germinates within 6 months, sometimes 12.

 Guadalupe Island, off the coast of California USA Zone 9 to 11

Guadaloupe Palm, Guadalupe Palm

Light- to deep-green leaves are 1.2–1.8m (4–6ft) wide, with spineless leafstalks about 1.5m (5ft) long. The leaflets taper, are slightly pendulous towards their ends, and segmented to about half their length. Sometimes there are more than 80 segments on each leaf. The flowers are clustered and followed by round fruits, 25mm (1in) wide, that mature to black and have a sweet, edible pulp. It has a deep-brown to dark-grey solitary trunk, 30–35cm (12–14in) in diameter.

Butia capitata

Butia Palm, Jelly Palm, Pindo Palm, South American Jelly Palm, Wine Palm

This fast-growing palm has variable leaf colour, mainly blue-green but also recorded as yellowish-green to silvery-green. Popularly known as one of the Feather Palms, its leaves are 2.4–3m (8–10ft) long. The flowers are yellow to orange and followed by yellow to light orange-red, round, sweet, edible fruits. It has a solitary grey trunk, up to 45cm (18in) in diameter.

 FACT FILE

 6–7.5m (20–25ft) in cultivation; taller specimens up to twice this height have been recorded in South America

 The head in mature palms is about 4.5–6m (15–20ft) wide

 Freely-draining but moisture-retentive soil and full sun encourage the best growth, although it is tolerant of drier conditions.

 It is often grown as a specimen palm in subtropical and warm-temperate regions. In these climates it is also ideal as a tub plant: position the container in full sun. It tolerates several degrees of frost and is one of the hardiest palms.

 Sow fresh seed; germination is slow but can be speeded up by nicking or cracking the seed's coat with a sharp knife or soaking seeds in warm water for a couple of days.

 Southern Brazil and northern Uruguay   USA Zones 8 to 11

A–Z PALMS

Calamus australis

FACT FILE

 18–25m (60–80ft) in the wild, where it uses its spiny stems to gain support from other plants, less in cultivation and especially when grown in a container

 3.6–4.5m (12–15ft), varies depending on its host (which can be any plant offering it physical support)

 Prefers fertile, moisture-retentive soil and full sun, although it thrives in partial shade when young. In ideal conditions, it grows moderately quickly.

 Young seedling plants have been used in bedding displays in tropical and subtropical regions.

 Sow fresh seed; when old it quickly loses its ability to germinate. Division of congested clumps is another way to increase this palm, but rooting and establishment are slow.

 North-east Queensland, Australia

 USA Zones 10 and 11

Hairy Mary, Lawyer Cane, Lawyer's Cane, Rattan Palm, Wait-a-while, Wait-a-while Palm, Wait-a-while Vine

This tall, somewhat scrambling, clambering and clustering palm has slim, flexible, spine-clad stems about 25mm (1in) thick. Light-green, narrow, leaflets, 30cm (12in) long, are borne on feather-like leaves up to 1.8m (6ft) long. They have a drooping and cascading nature. The flower-bearing stem is long and spiny; flowers do not usually appear until the uppermost part reaches the top of the forest canopy and enjoys full sun.

Carpentaria acuminata

(Kentia acuminata)
Carpentaria Palm

Emerald-green, narrow leaflets, lightly bluish-green beneath, are about 60cm (2ft) long, forming leaves that are 3–3.6m (10–12ft) long. They are borne on short leafstalks, while the leaflets arise in a V-shape formation from the central stem of each leaf. The leaflets have a limp nature, which complements the radically arching nature of the leaves. White flowers are followed by round fruits, which become scarlet when ripe. The solitary grey trunk of this moderately fast-growing palm is prominently ringed and 20cm (8in) in diameter.

FACT FILE

 15–18m (50–60ft) in the wild, less in cultivation

 3.6–4.5m (12–15ft)

 In its native area it grows in rain forests and alongside rivers, so in cultivation it needs a rich soil that remains moist. It grows in light shade when young, but later full sunlight encourages better growth. Outdoors it requires a tropical climate.

 In subtropical and warm-temperate climates it has been used in conservatories or, when young, as a houseplant, which needs good light. Warmth is essential, as is compost that does not become dry. When used as a garden feature, plant in small groups.

 Sow fresh seed, which germinates within 8–10 weeks.

 Northern Territory, Australia

 USA Zones 10b and 11

Caryota mitis

FACT FILE

 6–9m (20–30ft) in the wild, sometimes more, but invariably less in cultivation

 It has many slender trunks and forms clumps up to 4.5m (15ft) wide

 Fertile, moisture-retentive soil is essential, in partial shade or full sun. A tropical climate is also required.

 In the tropics it is often grown to form a hedge or screen. In temperate climates it is used as a houseplant; although it tolerates low light, it is best if given good light, fertile compost and adequate water. In tropical and subtropical regions it is often grown outdoors in tubs: position it in full sun.

 Sow fresh seeds (which are caustic); some germinate readily, although others take several months. Alternatively, divide congested plants.

 Wide area, embracing southeast Asia, but specifically the Philippines, southern China, Nicobar and Andaman Islands, Burma, Thailand, Malay Peninsula, Sumatra, Borneo and Java

 USA Zones 10b and 11

Burmese Fishtail Palm, Clustered Fishtail Palm, Fishtail Palm, Tukas, Tufted Fishtail Palm

This fast-growing palm has distinctive leaves, with wedge-shaped, ragged edged, mid-green leaflets that reveal a fishtail nature. The top is not well covered with leaves, but they create a dense screen at the sides. Flowering stems produce small, whitish flowers, followed by small, round, deep-red fruits that mature to black. The flesh is caustic. Flowering begins towards the top of a stem, proceeding downward until the lowest one flowers and the stem dies. It has a clustering, clump-forming nature, with many stems.

Caryota urens

Fishtail Palm, Jaggery Palm, Kitul Tree, Kittul, Kittul Tree, Sago Palm, Solitary Fishtail Palm, Toddy Palm, Wine Palm

This is a fast-growing palm when given ideal conditions. Glossy, dark-green, fishtail-shaped leaflets, up to 30cm (12in) long, are borne on leaves that are 3.6m (12ft) long, with 60cm (2ft) long leafstalks. Whitish flowers first appear towards the top of the palm, then slowly descend. Later the stem dies. The flowers are followed by round, dark-red fruits, 12mm (½in) wide, with caustic flesh.

FACT FILE

 12m (40ft), sometimes more, in the wild (less in cultivation), with a trunk of about 30cm (12in) wide

 The head in older palms is about 6m (20ft) across

 Fertile, moisture-retentive but well-drained soil is needed, in full sun or partial shade.

 In tropical and subtropical regions it is grown as a tub plant, positioned in full sun. Occasionally, in temperate climates, it is grown as a houseplant, which needs good light — especially in winter.

 The old stems are a source of sago, while the leaves yield a coarse fibre for making brushes. Young, tender leaves are eaten raw. This palm is best known for its sweet sap from unopened flowerstalks, known as toddy. After boiling, it yields a brown sugar, or jaggery; when fresh it is known as 'sweet toddy' while on becoming sour it is called 'fermented toddy', which is intoxicating.

 Sow fresh seeds (which are caustic); some germinate readily, although others take several months.

 India, Sri Lanka and the Malay Peninsula

 USA Zones 10b and 11

A–Z PALMS

Ceroxylon quindiuense

FACT FILE

 45–60m (150–200ft) in the wild, and claimed to be the tallest of all palms; invariably a lot less in cultivation

 The head on older palms is 6m (20ft) across, or more

 Cool, moist climates are essential; it does not survive in warm climates and especially where the temperature does not fall at night. In its native area it enjoys good light.

 Sow fresh seed, which germinates within 8–12 weeks.

 The trunk is covered with once commercially important wax.

 Andean region of Colombia

 USA Zone 9

Andean Wax Palm, Wax Palm

Dark-green leaflets, white or yellowish-grey beneath, are borne on ascending leaves that are 4.5–5.4m (15–18ft) long. It has a slow-growing nature. Large, distinctive clusters of flowers are followed by orange-red fruit when ripe. The solitary trunk, rarely swollen at its base, is straight, columnar, whitish-grey and has a thin coating of wax.

Chamaedorea cataractarum

Cascade Palm, Cat Palm, Cataract Palm

This trunkless, clustering, moderately fast-growing palm has leaves that are 1.2m (4ft) long and formed of dark-green, shiny, narrow and lance-shaped leaflets about 30cm (12in) long. The leaves have an attractive arching nature. The small yellow flowers are borne in clusters up to 45cm (18in) long and followed by round, red to black fruits, 12mm (½in) wide.

FACT FILE

 1.5–1.8m (5–6ft)

 Clump-forming to 3m (10ft)

 In its native areas it grows alongside streams in rain forests, so is best grown in fertile, moisture-retentive but well-drained soil. A warm climate and full sun are needed for rapid growth, but it tolerates light shade.

 Sometimes used as groundcover or as a dense hedge or screen in warm climates. In tropical, subtropical and warm-temperate climates it is grown outdoors as a tub plant: position the container in light shade. As a house-plant it needs good light, but tolerates light shade.

 Sow fresh seed, which germinates within 12 weeks, occasionally longer. Alternatively, clumps can be divided.

 Mexico

 USA Zones 10 and 11

A–Z PALMS

Chamaedorea elegans

(Chamaedorea humilis, Collinia elegans, Neanthe bella)
Good Luck Palm, Parlor Palm, Parlour Palm

This moderately fast-growing palm has light- to dark-green leaflets, up to 20cm (8in) long, on leaves 45–90cm (1½–3ft) long. Tiny, bright-yellow flowers are borne on upright branches and stems, followed by small, round fruits, first green then black. The solitary stem is light green and up to 25mm (1in) wide, with closely positioned dark-green rings that may lighten with age.

 1.8–3m (6–10ft) in the wild, but invariably less in cultivation, especially when grown indoors or in a greenhouse or conservatory

 The head in older palms is seldom more than 1.5m (5ft) across, usually less

 In its native area it is found in rain forests, where the air is warm and humid; if these conditions can be replicated in subtropical or warm-temperate climates, it is also successful outdoors. It tolerates light shade, though growth will be reduced.

 It is one of the easiest palms to grow, and perhaps the most popular indoor palm in temperate climates. In subtropical and warm-temperate regions it is often grown as a tub plant outdoors: position the container in light shade. It is also often grown to create groundcover in subtropical and warm-temperate regions.

 Sow fresh seed, which germinates within 12 weeks, occasionally longer.

 Southern Mexico and Guatemala

 USA Zones 10b to 11

Chamaedorea erumpens

Bamboo Palm

Deep-green, broad leaflets with a leathery texture are borne on many slim, bamboo-like stems. This moderately fast-growing palm has a clump-forming, spreading nature. It is often associated with *Chamaedorea seifrizii*, which has narrower leaflets. Despite claims from botanists that they are the same species, they are sold as distinctive and separate palms.

FACT FILE

 3m (10ft) in the wild, but invariably lower in cultivation

 60–90cm (2–3ft) and spreading

 It needs fertile, moisture-retentive but well-drained soil in light shade.

 It is widely grown in temperate climates as a houseplant, which needs light shade; it is also ideal for conservatories. In tropical and subtropical regions it is grown as a tub plant outdoors: position it in light shade.

 Sow fresh seed, which germinates within 12 weeks, occasionally longer.

 Guatemala and Honduras

 USA Zones 10b and 11

A–Z PALMS

Chamaedorea metallica

 1.8–2.4m (6–8ft) in the wild, less in cultivation

 1.2–1.5m (4–5ft) in the wild, less in cultivation

 Fertile, moisture-retentive soil and light shade suit it best.

 It tolerates low light and is widely grown as a houseplant in temperate climates: position in light shade. In subtropical and warm-temperate regions it can be grown outdoors in tubs: position the container in shade. It is a very adaptable palm and can also be used to create groundcover.

 Sow fresh seed, which germinates within 12 weeks, occasionally longer.

 Southern Mexico

 USA Zones 10b and 11

Metallic Palm, Miniature Fishtail Palm

Deep blue-green leaves with a distinctive metallic sheen are somewhat oval, but with a fishtail-shaped piece cut out of the top. Each leaf is borne on a 7.5–15cm (3–6in) leafstalk that holds the leaf more or less upright. Grooves in the leaves create an illusion of changing colour shades within a leaf. Deep-yellow flowers are followed by small, round, black fruits. This moderately fast-growing palm has a solitary trunk about 12mm (½in) wide.

Chamaedorea microspadix

Bamboo Palm, Hardy Bamboo Palm

This moderately fast-growing, clustering, clump-forming palm has dark-green leaflets, 20–25cm (8–10in) long and silvery-green beneath. The arching leaves are up to 60cm (2ft) long. Small, whitish-yellow flowers are followed by fruits that are 12mm (½in) wide and ripen to scarlet or deep orange. The individual stem-like trunks are 12mm (½in) wide.

FACT FILE

 3–3.6m (10–12ft), invariably less in cultivation

 1.8–2.4m (6–8ft); forms a clump

 Moisture-retentive but well-drained soil and light shade, preferably in a sub-tropical area, suit it best; it can also be planted in warm-temperate climates. Even when damaged by cold, it usually produces fresh shoots. it tolerates cold and frost.

 Often used as an architectural landscape palm in subtropical and warm-temperate climates. It is also used to create a screen or hedge. In warm climates it is used as a tub plant on a patio or terrace: position in light shade to good light.

 Sow fresh seed, which germinates within 12 weeks, occasionally longer.

 Eastern Mexico

 USA Zones 9 and 10

A–Z PALMS

Chamaedorea seifrizii

FACT FILE

 3–3.6m (10–12ft) in the wild, usually slightly less in cultivation

 90cm–1.2m (3–4ft), sometimes 1.8m (6ft) in the wild

 Fertile, moisture-retentive soil in light shade is required.

 In tropical and subtropical areas it is used to create hedges 1.2–1.5m (4–5ft) high. In temperate climates it is used as a large feature in a conservatory or as a house-plant, where it grows well in light shade to good light. In tropical and subtropical areas it can be planted in tubs outdoors: position it in light shade.

 Sow fresh seed, which germinates within 12 weeks, occasionally longer.

 Yucatán, Belize, northern Guatemala, parts of Honduras

 USA Zones 10b and 11

Bamboo Palm, Reed Palm

Deep-green, narrow leaflets, usually 20cm (8in) long, are borne on leaves with 5cm (2in) leafstalks. The 90cm (3ft) leaves appear at the tops of cane-like stems. The whole plant has a clump-forming, spreading nature. This moderately fast-growing palm is often associated with *Chamaedorea erumpens*, which has wider leaflets, though they are invariably sold as distinctive and separate plants.

Chamaedorea stolonifera

Mid-green, somewhat broadly lance-shaped leaves, 25–30cm (10–12in) long, are borne on 5cm (2in) leafstalks. This moderately fast-growing palm has a clustering, spreading nature, with underground stems (stolons) that spread to form clumps. Occasionally, in damp, humid, shady conditions, stolons appear above the soil's surface. The stems are only 6mm (¼in) in diameter.

FACT FILE

 1.8–2.1m (6–7ft) in the wild, less in cultivation

 Clustering nature; recorded as forming clumps up to 7.5m (25ft) across

 Fertile, moisture-retentive soil and light shade are required, as are tropical and subtropical conditions. It makes an excellent houseplant, tolerating low light.

 In the tropics and subtropics it has been used as groundcover, while in temperate climates it is frequently used as a houseplant: position in light shade to partial shade.

 Sow fresh seed, which germinates within 12 weeks, occasionally longer. It can also be divided.

 Mexico

 USA Zones 9 and 10

A–Z PALMS

Chamaerops humilis

FACT FILE

 1.8–6m (6–20ft), usually lower in the wild and forming a clump, but taller in cultivation when it sometimes has a solitary trunk with a diameter up to 30cm (12in)

 Mature clumps can be 7.5m (25ft) or more wide but, if there is a solitary trunk, the head is 3–3.6m (10–12ft) wide

 Slow-growing and able to tolerate occasional temperatures down to -9°C (15°F) in dry climates. Clump-forming types, with their larger canopy of leaves, are reported to be able to survive even lower temperatures. Outdoors, it thrives in well-drained, but not arid, soil and full sun. Indoors, it prefers soil-based rather than peat-based compost.

 In subtropical regions it is occasionally used to create low, informal hedges and screens, or planted as a decorative feature. It is ideal for planting in large outdoor tubs in warm-temperate and subtropical areas: position the container in full sun. It is also grown as a houseplant, especially in temperate climates, but bright light is essential to prevent plants from deteriorating.

 Sow fresh seeds, which germinate in 6–10 weeks. Alternatively, suckers can be removed and inserted in equal parts moist peat and sharp sand. Suckers rarely survive, and seeds are more reliable.

 One of the most northerly palms, native to a wide area; grows naturally along the coasts of western Mediterranean countries, the Atlas Mountains in Morocco, Malta, Sicily, Sardinia

 USA Zone 9

European Fan Palm, Fan Palm, Mediterranean Fan Palm

Fan-shaped leaves, 60–90cm (2–3ft) wide, are usually green but can be shades of bluish-green and greyish-green on some plants. Leaflets are stiff, narrow and tapering to about two-thirds of their length, with leaves borne on spine-clad leafstalks up to 1.5m (5ft) long. Erect clusters of yellow flowers are followed by round, small, yellow-orange or brown fruits.

Coccothrinax argentata

Florida Silver Palm, Silver Palm, Silver Thatch Palm, Silvertop, Silver Top Palm

This very slow-growing palm has circular to half-circular leaves about 90cm (3ft) wide. The leaflets are shiny and deep green above and silver to a metallic brownish-green beneath. They are borne on 60cm (2ft) leafstalks. The flowers are yellowish-white and followed by round purple fruits, 12mm (½in) wide. It has a solitary trunk about 15cm (6in) wide, with the upper part matted in dark brown fibres.

FACT FILE

 6m (20ft) in the wild, less in cultivation

 The head in older palms is about 1.8m (6ft) across

 Well-drained but moisture-retentive soil and full sun suit it. It survives cool areas, but the soil must be well drained throughout the year. It is tolerant of salt spray in coastal areas.

 Creates a spectacular feature when in a group in a tropical or subtropical garden, where it is also suitable as a tub plant: position in full sun.

 Sow fresh seed, which germinates within 12–15 weeks, sometimes longer.

 Southern Florida and the Bahamas

 USA Zones 10 and 11

A–Z PALMS

Coccothrinax crinita

FACT FILE

 7.5–9m (25–30ft) in the wild, less in cultivation

 1.8–2.4m (6–8ft), often less

 This slow-growing palm requires well-drained soil, bright sunshine and warmth in a tropical or subtropical region. It can survive considerably dry soil, but will not flourish in such conditions.

 Sometimes planted in small groups in an informal, ornamental landscape.

 Sow fresh seed, which usually germinates within 12–15 weeks, sometimes longer.

 Cuba

 USA Zones 9b to 11

Mat Palm, Old Man Palm, Old Man Thatch Palm, Palma Petate, Thatch Palm

Shiny green, rigid, narrow and tapered segments, silvery-green beneath, form circular leaves about 1.5m (5ft) wide. Borne on 1.2m (4ft) leaf-stalks, each leaf has about 50 segments. Yellow flowers are followed by round fruits, 25mm (1in) wide, that mature to black. It has a solitary trunk, about 25cm (10in) wide, cloaked in long, brown fibres.

Coccothrinax spissa

Guano, Swollen Silver Thatch

Semi-circular leaves are formed of light- to deep-green drooping and finely divided segments. They are grey beneath and form a rather sparse crown. The yellow flowers are followed by round deep-purple fruits 12mm (½in) wide. It has a slow-growing nature. The light-coloured, smooth trunk, 20–30cm (8–12in) wide, is often slightly swollen in its middle.

FACT FILE

 6–9m (20–30ft)

 1.8–2.4m (6–8ft)

 In its native area it grows in forest clearings, so in cultivation is best given moisture-retentive but well-drained soil in a sunny or lightly shaded position.

 Sometimes it is planted in an informal, ornamental landscape; it is suitable for planting in lax, well-spaced small groups.

 Sow fresh seed, which usually germinates within 12–15 weeks, sometimes longer.

 Dominican Republic

 USA Zones 10 and 11

Cocos nucifera

FACT FILE

 21–25m (70–80ft)

 The head in mature palms is 7.5–9m (25–30ft) across

 Well-drained but moisture-retentive soil produces the best plants, although it succeeds in poor soils. Good light is essential. Once established, it survives in relatively dry soil.

 In temperate climates it is occasionally offered for sale in pots for growing as a decorative feature, but usually dies within a few months as it is a tropical palm not suited to temperate climates.

 Often planted in vacation areas to create a tropical island atmosphere. Commercially one of the most widely cultivated palms, its fruits yield coconut oil. When fresh, kernels are shredded into desiccated coconut for confectionery. The husk yields coir-fibre for mats, brushes and ropes. The sweet juice is known as toddy when fresh; when fermented and distilled, it yields arrack, a strong alcoholic spirit.

 It is increased in the tropics, where temperature and humidity are high, by laying coconuts on their sides in warm, nursery beds and almost covering them with soil. Germination takes 3–6 months; in 10 months the seedlings, with nuts attached, are planted out into their growing positions.

 Thought to be the South Pacific, but now colonized in many coastal tropical and subtropical areas

 USA Zones 10b and 11

Coco Palm, Coconut, Coconut Palm

Leaf colour ranges from deep green to yellowish-green, with 90cm (3ft) leaflets on leaves 6m (20ft) long and borne on yellowish leafstalks that are 90cm–1.2m (3–4ft) long. This fast-growing palm begins flowering at an early age, with tightly packed white to near-yellow flowers. These are followed by the familiar coconut, 30cm (12in) long, yellow or green at first, becoming brown when ripe. It has a solitary grey trunk, about 30cm (12in) wide and with a slight bulge at its base. Some trunks curve and lean, especially when in coastal areas and exposed to prevailing wind.

Copernicia baileyana

Bailey Fan Palm, Bailey's Copernicia Palm, Yarey, Yarey Hembra, Yareyon

Light- to deep-green, stiff leaflets – often greyish-green beneath – form fan-shaped leaves about 1.5m (5ft) wide. They are coated in a waxy bloom and borne on 1.2m (4ft) toothed leafstalks. Branched clusters of whitish flowers are followed by brown to black, rounded fruits 25mm (1in) wide. This slow-growing palm has a smooth, solitary trunk about 60cm (2ft) wide, although the base at ground level is sometimes slightly swollen.

FACT FILE

 15–18m (50–60ft) in the wild; when grown decoratively the height is usually 9–12m (30–40ft)

 The head in older palms is 4.5–6m (15–20ft) across

 Well-drained but moisture-retentive soil and full sun are essential. In its native Cuba is grows in open woodland and savannas.

 In the tropics it is ideal for planting as a specimen palm, perhaps on a large lawn, and is at its best when planted in a small group.

 Sow fresh seed, which germinates in 3–6 months, but the seedlings develop very slowly.

 Cuba

 USA Zones 10 and 11

A–Z PALMS

Copernicia macroglossa

<table>
<tr><td>

FACT FILE

</td><td>

Cuban Petticoat Palm, Jata de Guanbacoa, Petticoat Palm

</td></tr>
</table>

 4.5m (15ft) in the wild, but in cultivation usually less

 The head in mature palms is up to 4.5m (15ft) across

 Well-drained but moisture-retentive soil and full sun are essential, in tropical or subtropical areas. It can survive in slightly dry soil, but will not flourish.

 It is an ideal palm for forming distinctive features in large lawns or borders in warm climates.

 Sow fresh seed, which germinates in 3–6 months, but the seedlings develop very slowly.

 Central and northwestern Cuba   USA Zones 10 and 11

Light- to deep-green, wax-covered, stiff leaf segments, greyish-green beneath, form wedge-shaped or half-circular leaves, 1.5–2.1m (5–7ft) wide. They are borne on short, toothed leafstalks. The leaves appear to form a dense skirt. The brownish-yellow flowers, borne in large clusters up to 1.8m (6ft) long, are followed by round, black fruits 12mm (½in) wide. The solitary trunk of this slow-growing palm, about 20cm (8in) wide, is smothered in old dead leaves. This gives the impression of a much wider trunk.

Corypha umbraculifera

Talipot Palm

The large, leathery, light- to dark-green leaves, up to 6m (20ft) wide, are claimed to be the largest on any palm. They are borne on stout 3m (10ft) leafstalks and armed with black teeth. The leaf segments are about 2.1m (7ft) long and 7.5cm (3in) wide. Creamy-white to yellow flowers are borne in large clusters and followed about a year later by dull-green fruits, 5cm (2in) wide. The trunks of mature palms are about 90cm (3ft) wide, and die after flowering. This is one of the largest flowering structures in the vegetable kingdom.

FACT FILE

 Mature palms grow 25m (80ft) or more high, but are usually seen at about half this height

 Mature palms have crowns up to 12m (40ft) wide, but are usually seen at about half this width

 This warmth-loving palm grows slowly when young, but moderately quickly once established. It needs fertile, moisture-retentive but well-drained soil in full sun. When established, it can survive in relatively dry soil.

 It is a massive palm unsuitable for planting in gardens, other than large-scale landscaping. In India and Sri Lanka it has been planted as a street tree to line wide roads, but only those with broad, grassed areas alongside them.

 The growing points were once used as a vegetable, and the large, ivory-like seeds as buttons and ornaments. The large, fan-shaped leaves have been made into *olas* (immature leaves bleached for use as paper). The leaves are used in the construction of umbrellas and in thatching, trunks are felled for the starchy pith, and the sap is used to make alcoholic drinks.

 Sow fresh seed, which usually germinates within 20 weeks, sometimes more.

 Southern India and Sri Lanka

 USA Zones 10b and 11

A–Z PALMS

Cyrtostachys renda

FACT FILE

 18–25m (60–80ft) in the wild, but in cultivation about 6m (20ft) or less

 The head is often 3m (10ft) wide and forms clumps 6–7.5m (20–25ft) across

 In the wild it grows in coastal swamps and lowland rain forest, so it needs moisture-retentive soil, full sun or light shade, high temperature and high humidity. It is moderate to fast growing when given full sun and plenty of water.

 It is ideal for growing in a tub on a patio in tropical regions: position the container in full sun.

 Sow fresh seed, which germinates in 8–12 weeks, sometimes longer.

 Malay Peninsula, Borneo, Sumatra and Thailand

 USA Zone 10

(Cyrtostachys lakka)
Lipstick Palm, Maharajah Palm, Pinang-rajah, Rajah Palm, Sealing Wax Palm

Light- to dark-green leaflets, light greyish-green beneath, are borne on leaves 1.2–1.5m (4–5ft) long, with 30cm (1ft) leafstalks. The feather-like leaves are stiffly erect. Small, greenish-yellow or greenish-white flowers are followed by black, round fruits, 12mm (½in) wide. This palm has multiple stems, 5–7.5cm (2–3in) thick, usually green, but light brown or even white in old palms. It has spectacular bright scarlet crownshafts.

Dictyosperma album

Common Princess Palm, Hurricane Palm, Princess Palm

Deep-green leaflets form leaves that are 2.4–3.6m (8–12ft) long. They are borne on 30cm (12in) leafstalks that have an attractive, twisting nature. The small, fragrant, creamy-white flowers change to reddish-brown and are followed by oval, deep-purple to black fruits, 12mm (½in) wide. There are several variations, for instance *Dictyosperma album* var. *aureum*, which has a yellow-orange stripe on the underside of its leaflets. The solitary trunk, 15cm (6in) wide, is grey, swollen at its base and has raised rings.

FACT FILE

 9–12m (30–40ft) in the wild, but less in cultivation

 The head in older palms is about 4.5m (15ft) wide

 Moisture-retentive soil is essential and although it survives in dry conditions it does not develop into an attractive palm. A tropical or subtropical temperature is essential, in full sun or partial shade. It grows moderately quickly if given optimum conditions.

 It is mainly grown in tropical regions, where it is used as an ornamental feature. In tropical and subtropical regions it is also grown as a tub plant on a patio, where it flourishes in full sun.

 Sow fresh seed, which usually germinates within 12 weeks, sometimes longer.

 Rodrigues Island in the Indian Ocean (one of the Mascarene Islands); few, if any, specimens are still found in the wild

 USA Zones 10b and 11

A–Z PALMS

Dypsis decaryi

FACT FILE

10.5m (35ft) in the wild, 6–7.5m (20–25ft) in cultivation

4.5m (15ft) on mature palms

This moderate to fast-growing palm needs well-drained but moisture-retentive soil in full sun or partial shade.

It is widely grown in the tropics and subtropics as a specimen palm, or as a tub plant outdoors: position the container in full sun. As a houseplant it needs light shade to full sun.

Sow fresh seed, which usually germinates within 8 weeks.

Southeast Madagascar

USA Zones 10 and 11

(Neodypsis decaryi)
Three-sided Palm, Triangle Palm

Greyish-green to bluish-green leaflets form leaves about 3m (10ft) long, stiffly upright but slightly arching outward at their tops. The leaves are borne on 30cm (12in) leafstalks. Small yellow flowers are followed by oval, greenish-yellow to white fruits. It has a solitary, dark-green, ringed trunk, 30–38cm (12–15in) in diameter, sometimes more.

Dypsis lutescens

(Chrysalidocarpus lutescens, Areca lutescens)
Areca Palm, Butterfly Palm, Cane Palm, Golden Cane Palm, Golden Feather Palm, Golden Yellow Palm, Madagascar Palm, Yellow Bamboo Palm, Yellow Butterfly Palm, Yellow Palm

This moderate to fast-growing palm has yellow-green to dark-green leaves, 1.8–2.4m (6–8ft) long, with light-green to yellow leafstalks. The yellow is especially apparent if the plant is in a sunny situation. The leaves have an ascending nature, then arching. Yellow flowers are borne in pendent, branched clusters, followed by yellow-orange to purple or black, oval fruits, each 18–25mm (¾–1in) long. It has a clustering, clump-forming nature, although mature specimens have trunks 5–7.5cm (2–3in) in diameter. Occasionally, it adopts a branching stance.

FACT FILE

 9m (30ft) in the wild, sometimes more, but much less when seen as a house or conservatory plant

 Clumps are often up to 7.5m (25ft) wide, with leafy heads 3.6m (12ft) across; as a house or conservatory plant its width is obviously much less

 Well-drained but moisture-retentive soil and a position in full sun suit it best, encouraging the best leaf colour. Indoors, use loam-based compost and position in good light and warmth.

 With its multi-stemmed and feathery nature, it is ideal for planting in tubs in tropical and subtropical regions: position in full sun. Also often planted to create hedges and screens. Indoors, it is widely grown in temperate climates as a houseplant or in greenhouses and conservatories, when it needs light shade to full sun, but avoid strong and direct sunlight.

 Sow fresh seed, which usually germinates within 8–10weeks. It can also be divided.

 Eastern Madagascar

 USA Zones 10b and 11

A–Z PALMS

Elaeis guineensis

FACT FILE

 15–18m (50–60ft) in the wild, but in cultivation usually 12m (40ft) or less

 The head in older palms is about 7.5m (25ft) wide

 In its native area it often grows in continually wet and swampy ground, so in cultivation it prefers rich, moisture-retentive soil, and full sun or light shade. It is only suitable for tropical and subtropical areas, where it grows moderately quickly in optimum conditions.

 This stately palm is ideal on large lawns; plant it in groups of 3–5. Preferably use specimens with different heights. It can be grown in containers indoors in temperate climates, but is not long-lived as it demands high temperatures and good light.

 For centuries the fruits have provided an important source of edible and soap-making oils. They are cultivated by the million in southeast Asia, where they are an important source of vegetable oil.

 Sow fresh seeds; germination is not rapid and sometimes takes 6 months, but this can be speeded up by soaking the seeds in water for a week, or cracking or nicking the seed coat.

 Tropical Central and West Africa

 USA Zones 10 and 11

African Oil Palm, Macaw Fat, Oil Palm

Its dark-green leaflets, about 90cm (3ft) long, have a drooping nature. The erect leaves, 4.5m (15ft) long, arch slightly towards their tips and are borne on spine-edged leafstalks, 90cm–1.5m (3–5ft) long. Densely packed whitish flowers are followed by clusters of oval fruits, 30cm (12in) wide, that mature to black. The trunk is solitary; young plants have trunks clothed in wedge-shaped leaf bases, while older palms have knobbly scars.

Euterpe edulis

Assai Palm, Jacara Palm

Light- to mid-green, tapering leaflets form leaves that are 3m (10ft) long and borne on 30cm (12in) leafstalks. The leaves have a somewhat feathery appearance. Small, whitish flowers are followed by round fruits, 12mm (½in) wide, that mature from dark purple to black. It usually has a solitary, 15cm (6in) wide, light-grey to brown trunk, but can be clustered, as seen in the photograph below.

FACT FILE

 7.5–9m (25–30ft) in the wild, less in cultivation; it can be clustered or solitary

 The head in older palms is about 4.5m (15ft) across

 Fertile, moisture-retentive soil and partial shade are essential for moderately fast growth. Constant moisture is vital, as is slightly acid soil.

 Forms a distinctive ornamental feature in tropical gardens, especially when planted in small, irregular groups. Grows moderately fast if given partial shade and moisture-retentive soil. As a houseplant, it needs light shade, but do not expect it to live for a long time indoors in a temperate climate.

 Sow fresh seeds. Germination is usually within 6 weeks if seeds are fresh. If they have become dry, immerse in water for 3–4 days before sowing.

 Coastal Brazil

 USA Zones 10b and 11

Hedyscepe canterburyana

FACT FILE

 7.5–10.5m (25–35ft) in the wild, less in cultivation

 4.5–5.4m (15–18ft), sometimes less

 In the wild it grows in well-drained soil. Fertile, moisture-retentive but well-drained soil produces faster growth when in cultivation. It does not like a hot climate and needs light shade, especially when young.

 It is ideal for planting in a tub outdoors in subtropical and warm-temperate regions; position in light shade. As a houseplant, it needs light shade.

 Raised from seeds, but germination is erratic and often takes more than a year.

 Lord Howe Island in the Tasman Sea, about 450 miles off the east coast of Australia

 USA Zone 9

(Kentia canterburyana)
Big Mountain Palm, Umbrella Palm

This rare, slow-growing palm has deep-green, stiff leaflets, pale green beneath and about 30cm (12in) long. They form leaves that are 2.4–2.7m (8–9ft) long and have a stiff, arching nature. The leaflets arise from the leaf stem in a V-shaped formation. Eggyolk-coloured flowers are followed by fruits, 5cm (2in) long, that mature to dark red. The solitary grey trunk is about 15–30cm (6–12in) in diameter.

Howea belmoreana

(Kentia belmoreana)

Belmore Sentry Palm, Curly Palm, Sentry Palm

Dark-green leaflets, 90cm–1.2m (3–4ft) long, form leaves that are 2.1–3m (7–10ft) long and borne on 90cm (3ft) leafstalks. The leaflets rise and form a V-shape formation. This slow-growing palm has a solitary, ringed trunk, about 15cm (6in) in diameter.

FACT FILE

 7.5–12m (25–40ft) in the wild, much less in cultivation

 The head in older palms is about 3m (10ft) across

 Moisture-retentive soil and partial or light shade suit it best.

 In subtropical and warm-temperate climates it can be grown outdoors in a warm, wind-sheltered position in full sun or light shade.

 Raised from seeds, but germination is erratic and occasionally takes up to 3 years. Providing warmth encourages more rapid germination.

 Lord Howe Island (about 450 miles off the east coast of Australia)

 USA Zones 10 and 11

A–Z PALMS

Howea forsteriana

FACT FILE

 15–18m (50–60ft) in the wild, but 9m (30ft) or less in cultivation and much less when grown indoors

 The head in mature palms is about 6m (20ft) across, but less in cultivation

 Moisture-retentive soil and partial or light shade suit it best.

 It is widely grown as a houseplant in cool, temperate regions, when it needs light shade; in fact, it tolerates low light well. It is ideal for growing in tubs outdoors in subtropical and warm-temperate regions: position the container in full sun or light shade.

 Raised from seeds, but germination is erratic and occasionally takes up to 3 years. Providing warmth encourages more rapid germination.

 Coastal areas of Lord Howe Island (about 450 miles off the east coast of Australia)

 USA Zones 10 and 11

(Kentia forsteriana)
Foster Sentry Palm, Kentia Palm, Paradise Palm, Sentry Palm, Thatch Leaf Palm

Dark-green leaflets form leaves that are 2.4–3.6m (8–12ft) long; they are borne on 1.2–1.5m (4–5ft) leafstalks. This slow-growing palm has a solitary, ringed trunk, about 15cm (6in) in diameter and swollen at its base.

Hydriastele wendlandiana

Florence Falls Palm, Latrum Palm

Yellowish-green to blue-green or deep-green, irregularly arranged, wedge-shaped leaflets form leaves about 1.5m (5ft) long, sometimes longer. It is a slow-growing, clump-forming palm, although sometimes solitary, with a trunk 15cm (6in) in diameter.

FACT FILE

 12–18m (40–60ft) in the wild, less in cultivation

 3–3.6m (10–12ft), usually less

 Moisture-retentive soil and full sun are essential, although during its infancy light shade aids rapid establishment. Warmth is essential and it is best grown in tropical or subtropical areas.

 Occasionally used as a specimen palm, when it is best grown in a group of three. In tropical and subtropical regions it is used as an outdoor tub plant: position it in light shade.

 Sow fresh seed; germination takes 8–12 weeks. Alternatively, clumps can be divided.

 Northern and northeastern Queensland and the Northern Territory, Australia

 USA Zones 10b and 11

Hyophorbe lagenicaulis

FACT FILE

 4.5–6m (15–20ft) in the wild, usually less in cultivation

 The head in mature palms is about 2.4m (8ft) across

 This slow-growing palm requires fertile, well-drained but moisture-retentive soil in tropical regions. It is soon damaged by low temperatures, and requires full sun.

 Frequently planted as an ornamental feature in warm climates. It can be grown as a tub plant outdoors in tropical and subtropical regions: position in full sun.

 Sow fresh seed; germination takes up to 12 weeks.

 Round Island in the Mascarene Islands of the Indian Ocean

 USA Zones 10b and 11

Bottle Palm

Deep-green, narrow leaflets form arching leaves, 1.8–3.6m (6–12ft) long, which are borne on 25cm (10in) leafstalks. The leaflets form a narrow, distinctive V-shape. Small, white flowers are followed by round fruits, 25mm (1in) wide, that ripen to black. The light-grey to dull-white trunk is distinctive, with a bulbous base of about 60cm (2ft) in diameter before it narrows.

Hyophorbe verschaffeltii

Spindle Palm

Glossy-green leaflets, dull green beneath, form leaves 1.8–3m (6–10ft) long. They have an arching nature initially, then cascading, with leaflets arising from each leaf's centre in a V-shaped formation. The spindle-shaped trunk, narrow at its base and at the crown, varies in width but is usually 25–45cm (10–18in). It is ringed by leaf scars.

FACT FILE

 6–7.5m (20–25ft) in the wild, usually less in cultivation

 3m (10ft) in the wild, slightly less in cultivation

 This generally slow-growing palm requires fertile, well-drained but moisture-retentive soil in tropical regions. Full sun and warmth are essential as it is soon damaged by low temperatures.

 It is frequently planted as an ornamental feature in warm climates. In tropical and subtropical regions it is grown as a tub plant outdoors: position it in full sun.

 Sow fresh seed; germination takes up to 12 weeks.

 Mascarene Islands in the Indian Ocean, where it is nearly extinct

 USA Zone 10a

A–Z PALMS

Johannesteijsmannia altifrons

 4.5–6m (15–20ft) in the wild, usually less in cultivation

 Often reaches a width of 4.5–5.4m (15–18ft)

 Fertile, moisture-retentive but well-drained soil, warmth, high humidity and partial shade are essential. It is therefore best reserved for planting in tropical regions.

 Sow fresh seed; germination is invariably erratic and may take 10–12 weeks, sometimes longer.

 Malay Peninsula, Southern Thailand, Western Borneo and Sumatra

 USA Zone 10

Diamond Joey

This slow- to moderately fast-growing palm is unlike most others, with light- to medium-green, glossy, diamond-shaped leaves, up to 3m (10ft) long and 1.8m (6ft) wide in mature palms. They are borne on 1.8–3m (6–10ft) leafstalks and edged with saw-like teeth, though in many ornamentally grown palms they are just 75cm (2½ft). Each leaf is attached to a separate stem that grows from ground level, and creates a rosette of up to 24 leaves.

Jubaea chilensis

(Jubaea spectabilis)
Chilean Wine Palm, Coquito Palm, Honey Palm, Honey Wine Palm, Little Cokernut, Syrup Palm, Wine Palm

Dull-green leaflets, light green or greyish-green beneath and about 60cm (2ft) long, form leaves 2.4–3.6m (8–12ft) long. They are borne on leaf-stalks 30cm (1ft) long. The purple flowers are followed by pendent clusters of round yellow fruits, 25mm (1in) wide. This slow to moderately fast-growing palm has a solitary grey trunk with a diameter of 1.5–1.8m (5–6ft). Some have a slight and gradual bulge in their trunks.

FACT FILE

 21–25m (70–80ft) in the wild

 The head in older palms is often 7.5m (25ft) wide

 It needs moisture-retentive but well-drained soil and a sunny position in warm-temperate climates. It is not suitable for excessively warm regions. Once established it is able to survive relatively dry soil.

 Although it is ideal for planting in a warm-temperate climate as a feature on a lawn, it is also one of the most cold-hardy palms.

 Earlier, many of these palms were cut down and the sugary sap removed to make palm honey. The sap was used to produce sugar and palm wine.

 Sow fresh seed; germination is difficult and sometimes takes 12 or more months, though some palm experts claim it usually takes 3 months.

 Central Chile

 USA Zones 9 to 11

A–Z PALMS

Jubaeopsis caffra

FACT FILE

 6m (20ft) in the wild, usually less in cultivation

 Mature clumps are 4.5–5.4m (15–18ft) wide

 Fertile, freely draining soil in full sun suits it best. It can survive in soil that is slightly dry, but will not flourish.

 Sow fresh seeds; germination is difficult and takes many weeks, and even then is erratic. Keeping the seedbed damp by using sphagnum moss helps to improve the speed and rate of germination.

 Near the coast of Pondoland in northeastern South Africa

 USA Zones 10 and 11

Pondoland Palm

Light- to medium-green leaflets, 90cm–1.2m (3–4ft) long, form leaves that are 3.6–4.5m (12–15ft) long and have a graceful, arching nature. They are borne on leafstalks 90cm–1.2m (3–4ft) long. Young leaves display their leaflets in a V-shaped formation, while mature ones have a more relaxed nature. Cream-coloured flowers are followed by round, yellow fruits 25mm (1in) long. This palm has a slow-growing, clumping, clustered nature, with several stems.

Laccospadix australasica

Atherton Palm, Queensland Kentia

Light- to medium-green leaflets form leaves about 1.8m (6ft) long and borne on leafstalks 90cm (3ft) long. The stems are erect but gracefully arch towards their tops. Cream-coloured flowers are followed by oblong, berry-like fruits that mature to bright red. It has a slow-growing and usually clustering nature with deep green stems, each up to 5cm (2in) wide, but is sometimes solitary, with a trunk 7.5m (25ft) high and 10cm (4in) in diameter.

FACT FILE

 3–3.6m (10–12ft), with clustered stems; solitary types are higher (*see* left)

 Eventually forms a wide cluster of stems

 It needs a moisture-retentive but well-drained soil and a cool position in partial shade. It is easily damaged by frost.

 In warm climates, it is widely grown as a house, conservatory or greenhouse plant, when it needs light shade. In tropical and subtropical regions, it is grown as a tub plant outdoors.

 Sow fresh seed; germination is not rapid, usually between 12–20 weeks. Alternatively, remove suckers.

 Rainforest of northeastern Queensland, Australia

 USA Zone 10

A–Z PALMS

Latania loddigesii

 10.5–15m (35–50ft) in the wild, usually less in cultivation

 The head in mature palms is about 3.6m (12ft) wide

 This moderately fast-growing palm needs well-drained but moisture-retentive soil and a warm, sunny, sheltered position in the tropics or subtropics. It can survive in slightly dry soil.

 It is occasionally grown indoors in temperate climates, but is not a long-term success unless high temperature and good light can be provided. Outdoors, it is best grown in subtropical climates.

 Sow fresh seed; it usually germinates within 8–15 weeks.

 Mascarene Islands in the Indian Ocean, where it is nearly extinct

 USA Zones 10b and 11

Blue Latan, Blue Latan Palm

Bluish-grey to silvery-blue, lance-shaped leaf segments form fan-shaped leaves 1.8–2.4m (6–8ft) wide; they are borne on tooth-edged leafstalks 1.2–1.8m (4–6ft) long. Small, yellowish flowers are followed by plum-shaped brown fruits, each containing three sculpted seeds. It has a solitary, slim, grey to brown trunk, about 25cm (10in) in diameter, and slightly swollen at its base.

Latania lontaroides

Red Latan, Red Latan Palm

Young leaflets have red veins and edges, but this changes when it is mature to dull deep-green above and light-green beneath. The leaflets form fan-shaped leaves, 1.5–2.1m (5–7ft) wide, which are borne on red leafstalks, 90cm–1.2m (3–4ft) long. Small, yellowish flowers are followed by large, plum-like fruits that mature to dark brown. This moderately fast-growing palm has a solitary, slim, grey trunk; it is approximately 20cm (8in) in diameter, and is slightly swollen at its base.

FACT FILE

 10.5–15m (35–50ft) in the wild, usually less in cultivation

 The head in mature palms is about 3.6m (12ft) wide

 Needs well-drained but moisture-retentive soil and a warm, sunny, sheltered position in the tropics or subtropics. It can survive in slightly dry soil.

 Occasionally grown indoors in temperate climates, but it is not a long-term success without high temperature and good light. Outdoors, it is best grown in tropical and subtropical climates.

 Sow fresh seed, which usually germinates within 8–15 weeks.

 Réunion in the Indian Ocean USA Zones 10b and 11

A–Z PALMS

Latania verschaffeltii

Yellow Latan, Yellow Latan Palm

This moderately fast-growing palm has narrow, lance-shaped, yellow or deep yellow-green leaflets. They form leaves that are 1.2–1.5m (4–5ft) wide. The leaves are borne on 90cm–1.2m (3–4ft) leafstalks that are bright yellow, dusted in white when young. The solitary, slim, grey trunk is about 25cm (10in) wide.

 12–15m (40–50ft) in the wild, less in cultivation

 The head in mature palms is 3.6–4.5m (12–15ft) wide

 Needs well-drained but moisture-retentive soil and a warm, sunny and sheltered position. It can survive in slightly dry soil.

 It is best grown in tropical and subtropical climates.

 Sow fresh seed; it usually germinates within 8–15 weeks.

 Rodrigues Island in the Indian Ocean USA Zones 10b and 11

Licuala grandis

Fan-leaved Palm, Palas Payung, Ruffled Fan Palm, Vanuatu Fan Palm

FACT FILE

 2.4–3m (8–10ft)

 The head in mature palms is about 2.4m (8ft) across

 Moisture-retentive but well-drained, fertile soil and partial shade in a tropical environment, where the humidity is high.

 Can be grown indoors in temperate climates, but is usually short-lived (it is hard to provide high humidity indoors). Outdoors, it is grown as a tub plant in tropical regions: position in light to medium shade.

 Sow fresh seed; germination is very slow and unreliable, taking up to a year.

 New Hebrides islands in the southwest Pacific   USA Zone 10b and 11

This distinctive, slow-growing palm has undivided but pleated, semi-circular to wedge- or diamond-shaped leaves that are shiny-green and about 60–90cm (2–3ft) wide. They are borne on 90cm (3ft) leafstalks. It has a slim, grey, solitary trunk about 7.5cm (3in) in diameter.

 1.8–2.4m (6–8ft)   1.5–2.1m (5–7ft)

Licuala orbicularis

 Needs fertile, moisture-retentive but well-drained soil in light shade. Shelter from strong wind is essential as leaves are soon damaged when blown about. A tropical or subtropical area is needed.

 Select a tropical position with care as this palm should not be dominated by other plants. Outdoors, it is sometimes grown as a tub plant in tropical and subtropical regions: position the container in light shade. As a houseplant, it needs light shade.

 Sow fresh seed; germination is very slow and unreliable, taking up to a year.

 Sarawak, northwest Borneo   USA Zone 10b and 11

Shiny, dark-green, circular leaves are about 1.5m (5ft) wide and 90cm (3ft) long. Each leaf is formed of segments fused along their edges and borne on leafstalks 1.5–1.8m (5–6ft) long; although strong, they are thin and willow-like. Whitish flowers are followed by round fruits, 12mm (½in) wide, that mature to red. The trunk is small and usually solitary. Occasionally, this slow-growing palm is trunkless.

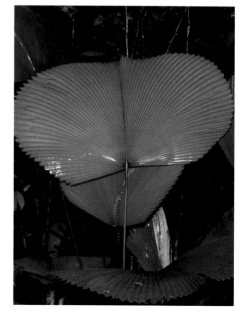

Licuala spinosa

(Licuala horrida)
Mangrove Fan Palm, Spiny Licuala

This distinctive, relatively fast-growing palm has shiny, mid-green, almost circular leaves radically segmented into 10–15 wedge-shaped segments. Leaves are 60cm (2ft) or more wide and borne on 90cm–1.2m (3–4ft) toothed leafstalks. Small, yellowish-white flowers are followed by pendulous clusters of small, round, red berries. The palm has clustering nature, with multiple, narrow but stiffly erect stems.

A–Z PALMS

FACT FILE

 6m (20ft) or more in the wild, slightly less in cultivation

 Mature clumps reach 4.5m (15ft) or more across

 It needs moisture-retentive but well-drained soil in partial shade or full sun. Although slightly hardier than many closely related palms, it is still only suitable for tropical and subtropical regions.

 It is sometimes used as an indoor palm in subtropical and warm temperate climates, where it needs light shade or full sun, but it is difficult for plants to survive for long periods.

 Sow fresh seed; germination is very slow and unreliable, taking up to a year.

 Malay Peninsula, Vietnam, Java, Borneo, western Indonesia, the Philippines, Thailand

 USA Zones 10 and 11

Linospadix monostachya

FACT FILE

 3.6m (12ft) or slightly more in the wild, less in cultivation

 In mature palms the head is 1.2–1.5m (4–5ft) wide

 This relatively slow-growing palm needs rich, moisture-retentive but well-drained soil in light shade in a warm climate. It is easily damaged by frost.

 It is ideal when young for growing as a houseplant in temperate climates, where it needs lights to medium shade. It is also grown as a tub plant outdoors in subtropical and warm-temperate regions: position the container in shade.

 Sow fresh seed, which occasionally takes 20 or more weeks to germinate.

 Dense rainforests of Queensland and New South Wales, Australia

 USA Zone 10

(Bacularia monostachya)

Walking Stick Palm

Deep-green leaflets form leaves 60–90cm (2–3ft) long; they are borne on 30cm (12in) leafstalks. Each leaf bears 10–20 leaflets. Arching flowers are followed by small, brilliant red fruits. It has a solitary light- to dark-green stem, about 25mm (1in) wide.

Livistona australis

Australian Cabbage Palm, Australian Palm, Australian Fan Palm, Cabbage Palm, Fan Palm, Gippsland Palm

Mid- to dark-green segments form circular to semi-circular leaves about 1.5m (5ft) wide. They are borne on toothed leafstalks 1.8m (6ft) long. The segments are split to half of their length. Small white flowers are followed by red or black fruits 12mm (½in) wide. It has a solitary, grey to dark-brown trunk about 30cm (12in) in diameter.

FACT FILE

 25–30m (80–100ft) in the wild, less in cultivation and usually only 12–15m (40–50ft)

 4.5m (15ft) when mature

 This moderate to fast-growing palm requires fertile, moisture-retentive but well-drained soil in full sun. It grows in a range of climates from tropical to warm-temperate zones, but when in cool areas the roots should not be in cold, water-logged soil. In its native areas it grows in swampy soil, as well as drier conditions.

 Widely grown as a specimen palm in warm areas, when it is best grouped with other palms, without intruding on its canopy. It is often used as a street tree. In subtropical and warm-temperate regions it is ideal as a tub plant outdoors: position the container in full sun. It can also be grown as a houseplant: position in light shade.

 Sow fresh seed, which germinates within 16 weeks.

 East coast of Australia, from central Queensland to Victoria

 USA Zones 9 to 11

Livistona chinensis

 12m (40ft) in the wild, usually less in cultivation

 5.4m (18ft) in mature palms

 This moderate to fast-growing palm needs fertile, moisture-retentive but well-drained soil in full sun, although it can survive in slightly dry soil. It grows outdoors in a range of climates, from tropical to warm-temperate zones, but when in cool areas the roots should not be in cold, water-logged soil.

 Widely grown as a specimen palm in warm areas, when it is best grouped with other palms, without intruding on its canopy. It is also used as a street tree in tropical and subtropical regions. It is grown as an indoor and conservatory palm in temperate climates, and as a tub plant in tropical, subtropical and warm-temperate regions: position in full sun or light shade.

 Sow fresh seed, which germinates within 16 weeks.

 Southern Japan, Ryukyu, Bonin Island and Taiwan; also claimed to be native to central China

 USA Zones 9 to 11

Chinese Fan Palm, Chinese Fountain Palm, Fan Palm, Footstool Palm, Fountain Palm

Bright, glossy-green leaf segments form circular or diamond-shaped leaves about 1.8m (6ft) wide and borne on 1.8m (6ft), toothed leafstalks. The segments are split to about half of each leaf's length. In mature palms, the head becomes packed with up to 50 leaves and forms a dense canopy. The solitary grey trunk (deep brown to reddish-brown when young) is about 30cm (12in) in diameter and often has an enlarged base.

Lodoicea maldivica

(Lodoicea sechellarum)
Coco-de-Mer, Double Coconut, Seychelles Nut

Glossy, deep-green segments form massive leaves, 5.4m (18ft) long and 3.6m (12ft) wide. They are borne on strong leafstalks, often 3.6m (12ft) long. The leafy crowns are formed of up to 20 leaves. Large, whitish flowers are followed by large seeds, often 38cm (15in) wide, 50cm (20in) long and weighing 18kg (40lb) – the largest and heaviest of any in the vegetable kingdom. These slow-growing palms do not flower under 30 years of age. They have a solitary, light- to dark-grey trunk, slightly bulbous at its base, and about 50cm (20in) in diameter. It is slightly ringed.

FACT FILE

 25m (80ft) or more in the wild, less in cultivation

 6–9m (20–30ft) in mature palms

 Well-drained but moisture-retentive soil, high humidity and partial shade in tropical regions suit it best.

 In its native areas it was earlier considered to have mystical qualities, while the seed was highly valued as an aphrodisiac.

 Sow fresh seed, which takes up to 18 months to germinate and is best sown in its growing position.

 Seychelles Islands in the Indian Ocean

 USA Zones 10b and 11

A–Z PALMS

Lytocaryum weddellianum

4.5m (15ft) in the wild, less
in cultivation, when it is usually
1.5–1.8m (5–6ft) high

1.5–1.8m (5–6ft) in mature palms

This slow-growing palm needs fertile,
slightly acidic, moisture-retentive but
well-drained soil in light shade.

Widely grown outdoors in subtropical
gardens as an ornamental palm, and as
a houseplant in temperate climates, where
it needs light shade and creates a highly
attractive plant with a feather-like nature.
In tropical and subtropical regions it is
ideal as a small tub plant outdoors:
position the container in light shade.

Sow fresh seed, which usually germinates
within 12 weeks, although longer times
have been recorded.

Coastal region of southeast Brazil; almost
extinct in the wild

USA Zones 10 and 11

*(Microcoelum weddelliana, Cocos weddelliana,
Syagrus weddelliana)*
Dwarf Coconut Palm, Sago Palm, Weddel Palm

Deep-green narrow leaflets, grey-green below, are 10–15cm (4–6in)
long, and form arching leaves that are 60–90cm (2–3ft) long. They are
borne on 30cm (12in) leafstalks. It has a solitary trunk, up to 10cm (4in)
in diameter, but usually much less. Elderly specimens become covered in
dark fibres, the remains of leaf sheaths.

Metroxylon sagu

Sago Palm

Dark-green leaflets, up to 1.5m (5ft) long, form leaves about 6m (20ft) long, sometimes more. The feather-like leaves, which are formed of leaflets in a V-shaped formation, initially have a well-defined upward nature, later arching at their tops. This palm has a clump-forming, suckering and fast-growing nature.

FACT FILE

 Stems up to 18m (60ft) have been recorded, but the usual height in cultivation is 7.5–9m (25–30ft), or slightly less

 2.4–3.6m (8–12ft), sometimes more when the leaves arch outward as they age

 Fertile, moisture-retentive soil and full sun are essential, as is a tropical environment. It is ideal for swampy areas.

 It creates a memorable feature, especially when 3–5 palms are in a group, but not tightly clustered together.

 Sow fresh seed; germination is slow and unreliable, taking up to a year. Removing sucker-like growths is a quicker and more reliable method.

 Southeast Asia

 USA Zone 10b

Normanbya normanbyi

FACT FILE

 15–18m (50–60ft) in the wild, less in cultivation

 4.5–6m (15–20ft) in mature palms

 This relatively fast-growing palm needs fertile, moisture-retentive, slightly acid soil, and a warm climate. Initially, it needs partial shade; later, it is more tolerant of high light intensities.

 It is sometimes grown as a specimen palm in warm countries; take care not to crowd it with other plants that impair its outline. In tropical and subtropical regions, it is grown as a tub plant for both sunny and shaded areas.

 Sow fresh seed, which germinates quite quickly, within 12 weeks.

 Northern Queensland, Australia; New Guinea

 USA Zone 10

Black Palm

Medium- to deep-green leaflets, bluish silvery-green beneath, form leaves 2.4m (8ft) long and with a characteristic arch. The leaflets arise at different angles to create a plumose and irregular feature. The leafy head is usually formed of 10 leaves on short leafstalks, while the pink to red, egg-shaped fruits, 5cm (2in) long, are borne in pendent clusters. The solitary, slim grey trunk is about 15cm (6in) in diameter.

Oncosperma tigillarium

Nibung Palm

Dark- to medium-green leaflets form elegant, feathery leaves 3m (10ft) long. Each leafy head is formed of up to 36 leaves, borne on 30–60cm (1–2ft) leafstalks. Bright yellow flowers are followed by small fruits, 18mm (¾in) wide, that ripen to black or dark blue, with a white bloom. This palm has a clumping nature with slim stems, initially light tan, covered in black spines. In aged specimens, stems 15cm (6in) wide have been recorded.

FACT FILE

 25m (80ft) or more in the wild, much less in cultivation

 Clumps are often formed of 40–50 stems, resulting in a width of 4.5–7.5m (15–25ft) in old specimens

 Moisture-retentive soil, warmth and sun are the prime requirements for rapid and healthy growth. It is only suited to the tropics and subtropics.

 It is an ideal palm for creating hedges and tall screens.

 Sow fresh seed, which germinates in 8–12 weeks. It is easier, however, to remove sucker-like growths; wear strong gloves and select small growths for best results.

 Malay Peninsula, Thailand, Java, Sumatra, Philippines, Borneo

 USA Zones 10 and 11

Parajubaea cocoides

Coco Cumbe, Coquito, Mountain Coconut, Quito Palm

Shiny, dark-green leaflets, 60cm (2ft) long and silvery beneath, are borne on leaves 3–3.6m (10–12ft) long and with 90cm (3ft) leafstalks. The leaves have an arching nature and the whole palm is reminiscent of the Coconut Palm, but faster growing and more tolerant of cool conditions. Small, dark-green fruits ripen to brown. The solitary, light- to dark-grey trunk is often 45cm (18in) in diameter and initially covered in dark, cinnamon-coloured leaf bases. It is slightly swollen at its base.

12–15m (40–50ft)

4.5–6m (15–20ft) in mature palms

This palm requires fertile, moisture-retentive but well-drained soil and a warm-temperate climate. It grows at high elevations and is not suitable for tropical culture. Full sun and cool nights suit it best.

It is widely planted as an ornamental palm in Mediterranean climates, as well as in its native areas.

Sow fresh seed; germination takes a long time so give seeds a pre-sowing treatment by soaking in water or nicking and cracking the seed coat. Alternatively, place them in warmth for about 6–8 weeks (up to 6 months is advised by some specialists) before sowing to encourage more rapid germination.

Ecuador and Colombia

USA Zones 9 and 10

Phoenicophorium borsigianum

(Stevensonia grandifolia)
Latanier Palm

Bright-green, arching leaves, about 1.8m (6ft) long, are borne on 25cm (10in) leafstalks that arise from the yellow-green midrib in a V-shape formation, but flatten with age. When young, the leaves appear to form large, undivided leaves, but they separate with age and buffeting from wind. Yellow flowers are followed by oval to heart-shaped fruits, 12mm (½in) long, that ripen to a dull red. It has a solitary grey trunk, about 10cm (4in) in diameter, that is smothered in spines when young.

FACT FILE

 12–15m (40–50ft) in the wild, less in cultivation

 3m (10ft) in mature palms

 Moisture-retentive but well-drained fertile soil and full sun are essential for this slow-growing palm. It is only suitable for tropical and subtropical regions with high humidity. Where possible, choose a wind-sheltered position.

 It is superb when planted as an ornamental palm in the tropics or subtropics, on its own or in a group. Ensure that other palms do not encroach on its outline. When young, it is grown as a tub plant outdoors in tropical and subtropical regions: position in light shade to full sun.

 Sow fresh seed; it takes 4–6 weeks to germinate if the seed is kept moist before sowing; if not, it can take about 10 weeks.

 Seychelles in the Indian Ocean

 USA Zones 10b and 11

A–Z PALMS

Phoenix canariensis

 15–21m (50–70ft) in the wild, less in cultivation and usually 10.5–12m (35–40ft) high

 Up to 7.5–12m (25–40ft) in mature palms, usually less

 Fertile, moisture-retentive but well-drained soil, full sun and a warm climate suit this moderate to fast-growing palm best. Like many other island palms, it tolerates salt spray. Once established, it can survive relatively dry soil. It will also tolerate a few degrees of frost.

 Frequently grown as an avenue palm in subtropical and warm-temperate regions. It needs plenty of space so avoid planting it where the lower leaves later have to be cut off, spoiling its shape. It is also widely grown in temperate climates as a houseplant: position in full sun.

 Sow fresh seed, which usually germinates within 4–12 weeks.

 Canary Islands

 USA Zones 9 to 11

Canary Island Date, Canary Island Date Palm, Canary Date Palm

Shiny, mid-green leaflets form leaves that are 3–6m (10–20ft) long, with a distinctive drooping nature in old palms and around the head's skirt. In mature palms, the head is often packed with more than 100 leaves. Small yellow flowers are followed by clusters of fruits that ripen to bright orange. The solitary, light- or dark-brown trunk is stout and upright; trunks in mature palms are 60–90cm (2–3ft) in diameter.

Phoenix dactylifera

Date, Date Palm

Greyish-green leaflets have a light-blue blush. They are 30–60cm (1–2ft) long and form leaves 3–6m (10–20ft) long. They are stiff at first, then slightly arching, but not cascading. The leaflets are attached to the leaf in a shallow V-formation. Mature palms often have 20–40 leaves; this is fewer than *Phoenix canariensis* and is one way to distinguish them at a distance. Whitish flowers are followed by large clusters of edible fruits, 2.5–7.5cm (1–3in) long. The trunk, usually covered in narrow, triangular leaf bases, is 30–45cm (12–18in) in diameter, although ones 60cm (2ft) wide have been recorded.

FACT FILE

 25–30m (80–100ft) in the wild, usually 15–18m (50–60ft) in cultivation

 6m (20ft) in mature palms

 This moderate to fast-growing palm needs moisture-retentive but well-drained soil and full sun. It tolerates sea spray, so grows in coastal areas. It is mainly planted in sub-tropical regions. Once established, it can survive relatively dry soil, but needs access to permanent ground water In cool areas, avoid excessive soil moisture.

 Similar to *Phoenix canariensis*, it is used as an avenue tree or ornamental palm, where it is best planted in small groups.

 Cultivated for more than 5000 years, few palms are better known. Male and female flowers are borne on separate plants. They produce fruits 4–5 years after planting, come into full bearing at about 15 years old and continue fruiting until 80 years. Fruiting bunches have about 40 strands of fruit, each with 25–35 dates. They yield 45–68kg (100–150lb) of fruit each year. These palms also yield a sugary sap that is boiled down to produce sugar, or fermented to produce palm wine (toddy).

 Sow fresh seed, which usually germinates within 12 weeks. It can also be increased by detaching sucker-like growths.

 North Africa, Middle East, Pakistan and northwest India

 USA Zones 7 to 11

A–Z PALMS

Phoenix reclinata

FACT FILE	

 9–15m (30–50ft) in the wild, 9m (30ft) in cultivation

 It has a clustering nature and may have 20–25 or more stems, forming a clump 10.5–13.5m (35–45ft) across

 This moderate to fast-growing palm needs moisture-retentive but well-drained soil in full sun. Best suited to tropical and subtropical areas, it can survive slightly dry soil.

 Occasionally it is used to create a tall screen or large hedge in subtropical regions, and in many warm-temperate regions where its clump-forming nature creates protection.

 Leaves are used for thatching and basket making, and wood from the trunks for construction work and making utensils.

 Sow fresh seed, which germinates within 12 weeks. Alternatively, it can be increased by detaching sucker-like growths.

 Tropical Africa, southern Africa, Madagascar, the Comoro Islands

 USA Zones 10 and 11

African Date Palm, African Wild Date Palm, Senegal Date Palm

Bright- to deep-green leaflets form leaves that are 3.6–4.5m (12–15ft) long and have a graceful, arching nature. Mature palms have 20–40 leaves. The edible, reddish-brown fruits are 12–25mm (½–1in) long. The multiple trunks are 10–18cm (4–7in) in diameter and, in older palms, covered in old leaf bases and brown fibres. Trunks invariably have a leaning and clump-forming nature.

Phoenix roebelenii

Dwarf Date Palm, Miniature Date Palm, Pygmy Date Palm, Roebelin Palm

The glossy-green leaflets, 25–30cm (10–12in) long, have a chalky bloom when young and form graceful, arching leaves, 90cm–1.5m (3–5ft) long. Light-yellow to white flowers are followed by small, black, oblong fruits about 12mm (½in) long. The solitary, erect trunk is 7.5–10cm (3–4in) in diameter, with triangular leaf scars. A clustering form is also known.

FACT FILE

 3m (10ft) in the wild, usually 1.8–2.4m (6–8ft) in cultivation

 3m (10ft) in mature palms

 Moisture-retentive but well-drained soil in tropical or subtropical regions suit this slow to moderately fast-growing palm best. In warm-temperate regions ensure that the soil does not retain excessive moisture (though in its native areas it is sometimes seen growing in areas that are occasionally flooded, and alongside rivers). Full sun encourages rapid growth.

 It is ideal for planting as a tub plant in tropical, subtropical and warm-temperate climates, where it needs to be positioned in full sun. As a houseplant it grows best in light shade to full sun.

 Sow fresh seed, which germinates within 12 weeks. It can also be raised by detaching sucker-like growths.

 Northern Laos, southern China, Vietnam

 USA Zones 9b to 11

A–Z PALMS

Phoenix rupicola

FACT FILE

7.5m (25ft) in the wild, usually less in cultivation

4.5m (15ft) wide in mature palms

It needs moisture-retentive but well-drained soil in full sun, in climates from tropical to warm-temperate. It can survive in slightly dry soil.

This decorative palm grows in sunny or lightly shaded positions. In tropical, subtropical and warm-temperate areas, it is grown outdoors as a tub plant: position it in full sun.

Sow fresh seed, which germinates within 12 weeks.

Himalayan India: Sikkim and Assam

USA Zones 10 and 11

Cliff Date Palm, Date Palm, East India Wine Palm, India Date Palm, Wild Date Palm

Glossy-green leaflets, 45cm (18in) long, form arching leaves that are 2.4–3m (8–10ft) long. The flowers are followed by yellow to orange fruits that mature to purplish-brown. The solitary trunk is about 25cm (10in) in diameter. It is moderate to fast-growing when grown in moisture-retentive soil.

Phoenix sylvestris

India Date, Khajuri, Silver Date Palm, Sugar Date Palm, Sugar Palm, Sugar Palm of India, Toddy Palm, Wild Date, Wild Date Palm

The grey-green to bluish-green leaflets, 45cm (18in) long, are borne on arching, slightly cascading leaves that are 2.4–3m (8–10ft) long. The leaves are plumose, with a spiky appearance. Whitish flowers are followed by large clusters of fruits that ripen to purplish-red. The solitary trunk is about 45cm (18in) in diameter; old specimens sometimes have their bases clustered with aerial roots.

FACT FILE

 12–15m (40–50ft), although taller specimens have been recorded

 7.5–9m (25–30ft), sometimes slightly more

 Although it survives drought, it is better when given fertile, moisture-retentive but well-drained soil, which encourages fast growth. It needs a position in full sun, both for growth and to enable the foliage to reflect its medley of colours. Once established, it can survive in relatively dry soil, but needs access to permanent ground water.

 Sometimes planted as a specimen palm in tropical and warm-temperate regions, both inland and in coastal areas.

 The sap is used to produce palm sugar and an alcoholic drink, while the fruits have been formed into a jelly.

 Sow fresh seed, which germinates within 12 weeks.

 India and southern Pakistan

 USA Zones 9b to 11

A–Z PALMS

Pinanga coronata

 6m (20ft) in the wild, less in cultivation

 Clumps up to 2.4m (8ft) in the wild, usually less in cultivation

 This moderately fast-growing palm needs fertile, moisture-retentive soil and light shade. Tropical or subtropical temperatures are essential.

 In the tropics or subtropics, it has been used to create screens, or planted in large tubs in courtyards and patios: position the container in light shade. As a houseplant it needs only light shade.

 Sow fresh seed, which usually germinates within 10–12 weeks.

 Indonesia

 USA Zones 10b and 11

(Pinanga kuhlii)
Bunga, Ivory Cane Palm, Pinang Palm

Light- to emerald-green, heavily veined, blunt-ended to pointed leaflets radiate from leaf stems at near 45-degree angles, forming leaves that are 90cm (3ft) wide and 1.2–1.5m (4–5ft) long. They are borne on 30cm (12in) leafstalks. Pinkish-white flowers are followed by fruits that mature to black. They have a clumping and spreading nature, with stems that are sometimes 5cm (2in) wide.

Pritchardia pacifica

Fan Palm, Fiji Fan Palm, Pacific Fan Palm

Brownish-green leaflets with a white, wax-like coating form circular leaves that are 90cm–1.8m (3–6ft) wide and borne on 90cm (3ft) leaf-stalks. Small yellow flowers are followed by fruits, 12mm (½in) wide, that mature to shiny black. The solitary grey trunk, ringed with old leaf scars, is about 30cm (12in) in diameter.

FACT FILE

 9–10.5m (30–35ft) in the wild, less in cultivation

 3.6m (12ft) wide in mature palms

 This slow-growing palm needs well-drained but moisture-retentive soil in full or partial sun. It tolerates salt-spray and is widely planted in coastal areas.

 Used in tropical and subtropical regions as a feature palm, in small groups or on its own, as well as a courtyard plant. It is ideal as a tub plant outdoors in tropical and subtropical regions: position it in light shade.

 Sow fresh seed, which germinates within 12–15 weeks, sometimes longer.

 Tonga Islands, later introduced to Fiji

 USA Zone 10

A–Z PALMS

Pseudophoenix sargentii

Buccaneer Palm, Cherry Palm, Florida Cherry Palm

Dark bluish-green, stiff, narrow and pointed leaflets, somewhat silvery beneath, form leaves 2.4–3m (8–10ft) long. The leaflets arise in a slight V-shape formation. There are usually about 12 leaves on each palm, initially slightly upright, then arching and splaying outward. Each leaf has a 60cm (2ft) leafstalk. Fragrant yellow flowers are followed by fruits, 12mm (½in) wide, that mature to deep red. This slow-growing palm has a solitary trunk, 30cm (12in) in diameter and tapering. There is usually a slight bulge half way up each trunk.

 7.5m (25ft) in the wild, slightly less in cultivation

 3–3.6m (10–12ft)

 Well-drained but moisture-retentive soil, full sun and warmth are essential, as is a tropical or subtropical climate. It can survive considerable drought.

 It is ideal for planting in ornamental landscapes, as well as in courtyards and around patios.

 Sow fresh seed, which usually germinates within 12 weeks.

 Bahamas, Cuba, Hispaniola, Belize, Mexico (Caribbean coast), Florida Keys

 USA Zones 10 and 11

Ptychosperma elegans

Alexander Palm, Solitaire Palm

The dark-green, tapering leaflets, 60cm (2ft) long, are light grey beneath and have jagged, cut-off ends. They form leaves that are 1.8–2.4m (6–8ft) long and borne on 30cm (12in) leafstalks. There are usually only 6–8 leaves on a palm at one time, although some specimens occasionally have up to 10. Initially, the leaves are upright, but soon have an attractive arching nature. White flowers are followed by oval fruits, 25mm (1in) long, that mature to bright red. The solitary light-grey trunk is about 10cm (4in) in diameter and ringed with the scars of fallen leaves.

FACT FILE

 9–12m (30–40ft) in the wild, less in cultivation

 3–3.6m (10–12ft)

 This fast-growing palm requires fertile, well-drained but moisture-retentive soil, warmth and partial shade or full sun, in tropical or subtropical regions.

 Because of its narrow nature it is often used where garden space is limited. When young, it is grown indoors in warm-temperate climates, but needs warmth, good light and regular watering to keep the compost moist.

 Sow fresh seed, which usually germinates within 15 weeks, sometimes slightly longer.

 Queensland, Australia

 USA Zones 10b and 11

A–Z PALMS

Ptychosperma macarthurii

7.5–10.5m (25–35ft)

Multi-trunked and clump-forming, possibly 6–7.5m (20–25ft) wide

Fertile, moisture-retentive but well-drained soil produces the best palms. It needs partial shade to full sun and a warm climate, from subtropical to tropical. In its native areas it grows in rain forests.

In tropical and subtropical areas it forms dominant, decorative clumps, creates large screens, or is planted in large tubs for decorating courtyards and patios: position the container in full sun.

Sow fresh seed, which usually germinates within 15 weeks, sometimes slightly longer.

Papua New Guinea and northeast Australia

USA Zones 10b and 11

Hurricane Palm, Macarthur Feather Palm, Macarthur Palm

Medium to bright deep-green, broad leaflets about 60cm (2ft) long, have ends that are jagged and appear to have been bitten off. They form leaves 90cm–1.8m (3–6ft) long, borne on short leafstalks – seldom more than 30cm (12in) long. Each leaf has 20 or more pairs of leaflets. Small yellowish-white flowers are followed by fruits, 12mm (½in) long, that mature from green to bright red. The multiple stems of this fast-growing palm resemble those of bamboos and are initially green, later grey.

Raphia farinifera

(Raphia kirkii, Raphia pedunculata, Raphia polymita, Raphia ruffia)
Madagascar Raffia Palm, Raffia Palm

Stiff, deep-green leaflets, bluish-green beneath, are 2.4m (8ft) long. They form erect, then slightly arching leaves, up to 18m (60ft) long. Each leaf has a stiff leafstalk, up to 6m (20ft) long. The massive, feather-like leaves are claimed to be among the longest in any terrestrial plant. The multiple or solitary trunks are 30cm (12in) in diameter, sometimes slightly more. As each trunk flowers and bears fruit, it dies and is replaced by others.

FACT FILE

 3–9m (10–30ft) in the wild, usually less in cultivation

 7.5–9m (25–30ft) on mature palms

 This is a fast-growing palm when given moisture-retentive soil and full sun. It grows well in swampy situations in the tropics.

 It is sometimes grown as a majestic feature in a large area in the tropics and subtropics, but needs to be seen from a distance for its grandeur to be appreciated.

 The leaf-bases were earlier used to make raffia fibre, widely used by gardeners and nurserymen for securing plants. Leaves are used to make baskets and for thatching, while juice from the stems produces a palm wine known as Harafa.

 Sow fresh seed, which usually germinates quickly, although occasionally takes 20 weeks or more.

 Tropical Africa, Madagascar

 USA Zone 10

A–Z PALMS

Ravenea rivularis

FACT FILE

 25m (80ft) in the wild, usually 10.5–12m (35–40ft) in cultivation

 3–4.5m (10–15ft) in mature palms

 Rich, moisture-retentive soil and light shade suit it best. It is ideal for growing in tropical, subtropical and warm-temperate climates. In its native area it grows in swamps and alongside rivers and streams.

 It is often planted as a specimen palm, either on its own or in a group of three. It is sometimes grown indoors or in conservatories in temperate climates, but ensure it is positioned in good light and the compost does not become dry. It is an ideal outdoor tub plant in tropical, subtropical and warm-temperate regions. In cool areas, position it in full sun.

 Sow fresh seed; germination takes up to 15 weeks.

 Madagascar

 USA Zones 10 and 11

Majesty Palm

Deep-green, 60cm (2ft) leaflets form leaves that are 1.8–2.4m (6–8ft) long. They have a distinctive, feather-like shape, initially with an upright stance, later slightly arching. They are borne on 30cm (12in) leafstalks. Small white flowers are followed by round fruits, 12mm (½in) wide, that ripen to a rich, bright red. The solitary trunk of this fast-growing palm is up to 30cm (12in) in diameter, with a slightly swollen base.

Reinhardtia gracilis

Window Palm, Window Pane Palm

Glossy-green, wedge-shaped leaflets – often with small holes, or 'windows', at their base – form leaves up to 30cm (12in) long. They are borne on thin, green, leafstalks that range in length from 7.5–45cm (3–18in). Small, whitish flowers are followed by fruits, 25mm (1in) long, that mature to black. It is usually clump-forming, with clustered stems that are about 25mm (1in) in diameter and mainly green. Occasionally, this fairly slow-growing palm is seen with a solitary trunk.

FACT FILE

 3m (10ft) in the wild, 1.2–1.5m (4–5ft) in cultivation

 Groups of clustered stems are up to 1.2m (4ft) wide

 Fertile, moisture-retentive but rapidly draining soil and light shade are needed. Outdoors, it is a palm for tropical and subtropical regions.

 Ideal in tropical and subtropical climates for growing in large containers on a lightly shaded patio or in a courtyard. It is sometimes grown indoors and in conservatories in temperate climates, but usually is short-lived because of the need for high humidity and light shade. It is grown as a tub plant in tropical and subtropical regions: position it in light shade. It is ideal for creating groundcover in tropical and subtropical regions.

 Sow fresh seed; germination is slow. Although it can be divided, seed remains the best method.

 Southern Mexico to Honduras

 USA Zone 10

Rhapidophyllum hystrix

FACT FILE

 3.6m (12ft) in the wild, usually 1.8–2.4m (6–8ft) high in cultivation

 1.8–2.4m (6–8ft) in established palms

 Rich, moisture-retentive but well-drained soil in light shade or full sun is needed. In its native area it often grows in swampy land.

 It has a hardy nature, being particularly resistant to cold. It is used to create an ornamental feature in lawns in warm-temperate and subtropical climates. Its suckering nature creates a dominant feature and it is especially attractive when young and relatively short. It is ideal for creating hedges and screens.

 Sow fresh seed; germination is extremely slow and claimed to be up to 2 years. Dividing congested clumps is an alternative, but they take a long time to become established.

 Southeastern North America, including southern Alabama, southwestern Mississippi, southern Georgia, Florida, South Carolina

 USA Zone 6 to 10

Blue Palmetto, Creeping Palmetto, Dwarf Saw Palmetto, Hedgehog Palm, Needle Palm, Porcupine Palm, Spine Palm, Vegetable Porcupine

Deep-green segments, green and silvery beneath, form semi-circular leaves about 1.2m (4ft) wide. Leaf segments are about 25mm (1in) wide, with 15–24 in each leaf. Each leaf is borne on an upright leafstalk, 90cm–1.2m (3–4ft) long. Yellowish-white flowers are followed by reddish-purple to brown fruits, 12mm (½in) wide, heavily dusted in white. This slow-growing palm has a short, distinctive trunk about 10cm (4in) in diameter, clad in vertical sharp, black spines 10cm (4in) or more long.

Rhapis excelsa

(Rhapis flabelliformis)
Bamboo Palm, Fern Rhapis, Ground Rattan, Lady Palm, Little Lady Palm, Miniature Fan Palm, Slender Lady Palm

Some 12–20, deep glossy-green segments, each about 23cm (9in) long, form near-circular leaves that are 45cm (18in) wide and borne on 45cm (18in) leafstalks. The end of each segment is squared or jagged. There are many attractively variegated cultivars, from 'Ayanishiki' (creamy-white stripes on its leaves) to 'Zuiko-Lutino' (broad creamy-white stripes). It is slow growing, with a clump-forming nature and slim, stiff stems up to 25mm (1in) wide.

FACT FILE

 3m (10ft) in the wild, less in cultivation

 1.2–1.5m (4–5ft), clustered and clumping, with a spreading nature

 Well-drained, neutral soil and light shade suits it best. It is claimed to survive temperatures as low as -6.6°C (20°F), but in such conditions avoid soil that retains moisture that may chill the roots. Even when stems are badly frosted the plant often rejuvenates itself, with further shoots arising from the roots.

 It is often planted outdoors in subtropical and warm-temperate climates where it forms an attractive, informal hedge. As a houseplant, as well as in conservatories and sunrooms, it needs light shade and will tolerate very low light. It is planted as an outdoor tub plant in subtropical and warm-temperate regions, where it thrives in sun or shade.

 Sow fresh seed, which germinates within 12 weeks. Usually, it is increased by dividing clustered clumps.

 Thought to have originated in China, but introduced into cultivation from Japan; unknown in the wild

 USA Zone 9b to 11

A–Z PALMS

Rhapis humilis

FACT FILE

3.6–6m (12–20ft), less in cultivation

1.2–1.8m (4–6ft), clustered and clumping, with a spreading nature

Well-drained, neutral soil and light shade are required.

Its clump-forming nature makes it ideal for forming a large hedge or barrier in subtropical and warm-temperate climates. In temperate regions, it can be grown as a houseplant, or in conservatories or sun-rooms, where it needs light shade. It is planted as an outdoor tub plant in sub-tropical and warm-temperate regions, where it thrives in sun or shade.

Increased by dividing clustered clumps and removing suckers.

Thought to be native to southern China, but unknown in the wild

USA Zones 8b to 11

Reed Rhapis, Slender Lady Palm

Many narrow segments, with pointed ends that form circular leaves 45cm (18in) wide, are borne on 45cm (18in) leafstalks. Its slow-growing, clump-forming nature produces slim stems.

Rhopalostylis sapida

Brush Palm, Feather Duster Palm, Nikau, Nikau Palm,
Shaving-brush Palm

Light-green, stiff, 60–90cm (2–3ft) leaflets, initially upright, form slightly arching leaves that are 4.5m (15ft) long and have a feathery nature. The leaflets arise in a V-shape. Fruits are bright red when ripe. This very slow-growing palm has a solitary, straight, smooth, green trunk, 23cm (9in) in diameter, with a prominently bulging crownshaft.

FACT FILE

 7.5–9m (25–30ft)

 6m (20ft)

 Needs well-drained but moisture-retentive soil and light shade. In its native area it grows in lowland forests. Outdoors, it is best grown in cool, subtropical or warm-temperate areas. Low temperatures damage it, especially if the soil is continually moist.

 In warm-temperate areas, it is sometimes planted as a specimen palm, or in a cluster of three. It is best grown in light shade. As a houseplant, it tolerates low light.

 Maoris used the leaves for thatching, and the growing point as 'cabbage'.

 Sow fresh seed, which germinates within 12 weeks.

 North and South Islands, New Zealand, and the Chatham Islands

 USA Zone 10

A–Z PALMS

Roystonea regia

FACT FILE

 25–30m (80–100ft) in the wild, less in cultivation

 4.5m (15ft)

 This fast-growing palm needs fertile, moisture-retentive soil and warmth in a tropical environment. Full sun is essential for rapid growth. In its native area it is often seen growing in swamps and alongside streams and rivers.

 It is frequently planted in tropical and subtropical areas as a specimen palm in large landscapes. If three are planted in a group, ensure the leaves do not touch; this spoils their distinctive outlines. It is also frequently used in these regions as a tub plant outdoors: position the container in full sun.

 Sow fresh seed, which usually germinates within 12 weeks, occasionally longer.

 Cuba (now widely spread in Central America, Mexico, Florida and the Bahamas)

 USA Zones 10 and 11

Cuban Royal, Cuban Royal Palm, Florida Royal Palm, Royal Palm

Deep-green, 60cm–1.2m (2–4ft) leaflets form feather-like leaves up to 3.6m (12ft) long. They are borne on 20cm (8in) leafstalks. The leaflets arise at irregular angles and create attractive features. White flowers are followed by reddish-brown fruits that mature to blackish-purple. It has a solitary, straight, smooth, light-grey to white trunk, 50–60cm (20–24in) in diameter, that is swollen and ringed at the base.

Sabal minor

(Sabal deeringiana, Sabal louisiana, Sabal minima,
Sabal pumila)
Blue Palmetto Palm, Bush Palmetto, Dwarf Palm, Dwarf Palmetto, Dwarf Palmetto Palm, Little Blue Stem, Scrub Palmetto, Swamp Palmetto

Dark-green or bluish-green, stiff, narrow leaf segments form fan-shaped leaves that are about 1.5m (5ft) wide and borne on leafstalks up to 1.5m (5ft) long, sometimes longer. Whitish flowers are followed by dark-brown to black fruits. It is usually clustered and trunkless, taller stems have been described in swampy native areas.

FACT FILE

 3–3.6m (10–12ft), sometimes shorter, although stems to 5.4m (18ft) have been recorded

 2.4–3.6m (8–12ft) clustered stems, usually without a trunk

 Grows slowly or moderately fast and needs fertile, moisture-retentive soil and light shade. In its native areas it is often seen in swamps, but can also survive slight dryness in the soil. It is very cold hardy.

 Best reserved for moist soil in a tropical or subtropical setting, rather than an ornamental garden. In tropical, subtropical and warm-temperate climates, it is grown as a tub plant outdoors: position the container in full sun.

 Sow fresh seed, which germinates quickly, usually within 6–8 weeks.

 Southeastern USA: Texas, Oklahoma, Louisiana, Mississippi, Alabama, Arkansas, Georgia, South and North Carolina, Florida

 USA Zones 6 to 11

A–Z PALMS

Sabal palmetto

FACT FILE

 18–25m (60–80ft) in the wild, much less in cultivation

 2.4–3.6m (8–12ft), sometimes more

 Grows slowly or moderately fast and needs fertile, moisture-retentive soil and full sun or partial shade. Grows best in swampy areas and alongside rivers and streams, but can survive in slightly dry soil. Tropical and subtropical areas are usually necessary, although it will survive (but not well) in warm-temperate areas if the soil is not continually moist.

 Best reserved for moist soil in a tropical or subtropical natural setting, rather than an ornamental garden. Plant in small groups.

 The leaves have been used for thatching and making baskets. The fruit is edible, and the water-resistant trunks have been used for piling.

 Sow fresh seed, which germinates quickly, usually in 6–8 weeks.

 Southeastern USA: North and South Carolina, Florida; the Bahamas; southern Cuba

 USA Zone 8 to 11

(Sabal viatoris, Sabal parviflora, Sabal jamesiana, Sabal bahamensis)

Blue Palmetto, Cabbage Palm, Cabbage Palmetto, Cabbage Tree, Common Palmetto, Palmetto, Palmetto Palm

Deep-green, stiff, leaf segments form leaves that are 1.5–2.4m (5–8ft) wide and borne on 1.8–2.1m (6–7ft) leafstalks. Fragrant white flowers are followed by oval, almost black fruits. The solitary, brownish to grey trunk can be 30–60cm (1–2ft) in diameter, usually less. It is generally covered in old leaf bases.

Serenoa repens

(Serenoa serrulata)
Saw Palmetto, Scrub Palmetto

It has variable leaf colour, including green and greyish-green to blue-silver and silvery-white. Semi-circular leaves, 90cm (3ft) wide, are borne on 90cm–1.5m (3–5ft) spine-clad leafstalks. Each leaf is formed of stiff, deeply divided segments. Small white flowers are followed by fruits that mature to black and have an unpleasant odour. This palm grows slowly or moderately fast. Trunks are very short, creeping or absent.

FACT FILE

 1.8–2.4m (6–8ft), usually less

 Creeping and branching stems, forming dense clumps, with roots spreading underground and appearing several metres away from the parent plant.

 Light, sandy, well-drained soil and full sun are needed. Although the soil must be well drained, it should retain some moisture.

 Forms an attractive groundcover, but is difficult to transplant and re-establish. Sometimes it is grown in a container in warm areas. It is ideal for creating a hedge or screen.

 Sow fresh seed, which usually germinates within 20 weeks, occasionally longer. Alternatively, divide congested clumps.

 Southeastern USA, especially the southern and coastal strips of Mississippi, Louisiana, Florida, Georgia, South Carolina

 USA Zones 8 to 11

A–Z PALMS

Syagrus romanzoffiana

FACT FILE

 12–21m (40–70ft) in the wild; unusually for most palms, it is often slightly higher in cultivation

 6–7.5m (20–25ft)

 It needs moderately rich, well-drained but moisture-retentive soil in full sun and a subtropical or warm-temperate climate. It is more tolerant of cold when the soil is relatively dry.

 Often planted as a specimen palm, it quickly creates a spectacular feature; growth rates of 75cm (30in) a year have been recorded. In tropical, subtropical and warm-temperate climates, it is grown as an outdoor tub plant: position it in full sun, especially in warm-temperate climates. As a houseplant it needs good light and for this reason is not always successful.

 A highly decorative palm often used as a street tree in warm climates.

 Sow fresh seed, which germinates within 15 weeks, sometimes less.

 Northeast Argentina, Uruguay, eastern Paraguay, southeast Brazil

 USA Zones 9b to 11

(Arecastrum romanzoffiana, Cocos plumosa, Cocos romanzoffiana)
Giriba Palm, Queen Palm

Light- to deep-green, sometimes slightly yellow, arching leaflets, 30–60cm (1–2ft) long, form arching leaves that are 2.1–3.6m (7–12ft) long. The 25mm (1in) fruits mature to yellow or rich orange. The solitary trunks are usually 45–50cm (18–20in) in diameter, but palms with trunks only 15–20cm (6–8in) diameter have been recorded.

Thrinax morrisii

(Thrinax microcarpa, Thrinax bahamensis, Thrinax drudei, Thrinax keyensis, Thrinax praeceps, Thrinax puntculata)
Brittle Thatch, Brittle Thatch Palm, Broom Palm, Buffalo-thatch, Buffalo Top, Peaberry Palm, Pimetta, Key Palm, Key Thatch, Silver Thatch Palm

This slow-growing palm has bluish-green leaf segments when young. Later they are darker green, with light-green undersides. They form rounded leaves, 60–90cm (2–3ft) wide, and borne on 90cm (3ft) leaf-stalks. The solitary trunk is about 20cm (8in) in diameter.

FACT FILE

 9–10.5m (30–35ft) in the wild, less in cultivation

 2.4–3m (8–10ft)

 It needs well-drained soil in full light in subtropical and tropical regions. It can survive considerably dry conditions.

 In tropical and subtropical regions it is sometimes grown as a tub plant: position the container in full sun. It is also planted as a street tree in these regions.

 Sow fresh seed, which germinates within 15 weeks, sometimes less.

 Florida Keys, Bahamas, Cuba, Puerto Rico, Lesser Antilles Islands of Anguilla and Barbuda

 USA Zones 9b to 11

A–Z PALMS

Thrinax parviflora *(Thrinax harrisiana, Thrinax tessellata)*

FACT FILE

 12–15m (40–50ft) in the wild, less in cultivation

 2.4–3m (8–10ft)

 This slow-growing palm requires well-drained soil in full light, in subtropical and tropical regions. It can survive considerable dryness in the soil.

 Sow fresh seed, which germinates within 15 weeks, sometimes less.

 Jamaica   USA Zone 10

Broom Palm, Florida Thatch Palm, Iron Thatch, Mountain Thatch Palm, Jamaica Thatch Palm, Palmetto Thatch, Thatch, Thatch Pole

Medium- to dark-green leaf segments form circular leaves that are 90cm–1.2m (3–4ft) wide. These are borne on 1.2m (4ft) leafstalks. The solitary trunk is 15cm (6in) in diameter.

 9–12m (30–40ft) in the wild, usually less in cultivation

 1.8–2.4m (6–8ft)

Thrinax radiata *(Thrinax floridana, Thrinax excelsa, Thrinax multiflora, Thrinax pumilo, Coccothrinax radiata, Thrinax martii, Thrinax wendlandiana)*

Florida Thatch Palm, Jamaica Thatch, Sea Thatch, Silk-top Thatch

 This slow-growing palm needs well-drained soil, in partial or full sun. It can survive considerable dryness in the soil.

 Ideal when young to create interest at eye-height and up to 4.5m (15ft). In tropical and subtropical regions, it is often grown as a tub plant: position it in full sun.

 Sow fresh seed, which germinates within 15 weeks, sometimes less.

 Florida Keys, western Cuba, Bahamas, Hispaniola, Belize

 USA Zones 10 and 11

Bright, medium-green leaf segments, greyish-green beneath, form fan-shaped, near-circular leaves that are 1.2m (4ft) wide and borne on 90cm (3ft) leafstalks. Each leaf is formed of about 50 segments. The trunk is usually solitary and about 13cm (5in) in diameter.

Trachycarpus fortunei

(Trachycarpus excelsus, Chamaerops excelsa, Chamaerops fortunei)

Chinese Windmill Palm, Chusan Palm, Fan Palm, Hemp Palm, Windmill Palm

Dark-green, irregular-sized leaf segments form fan-shaped leaves that are 90cm–1.2m (3–4ft) wide and borne on 45–60cm (1½–2ft) leaf-stalks. Yellow flowers are followed by small, kidney-shaped fruits that ripen to blue-black and are covered with an attractive white bloom. The solitary trunk is 20–25cm (8–10in) in diameter and covered with pale-brown fibres.

A–Z PALMS

FACT FILE

 12–15m (40–50ft), usually less

 1.8–3m (6–10ft), sometimes slightly more

 Well-drained but moisture-retentive soil and full sun are ideal, but avoid very strong and direct sunlight. This palm generally has a fast-growing nature, though its growth decreases during its latter years. It prefers a wind-sheltered position. It is very cold hardy and commonly seen in UK and European gardens.

 Often planted individually or in a small group (but without the leaves touching) in a wind-sheltered ornamental area. In subtropical and warm-temperate climates, it is grown as an outdoor tub plant: position it in full sun. In these regions it is also planted as a street tree, or grown as a houseplant, when it needs good light.

 Fibres around the trunk are used to make cordage and brushes, and the leaves to make hats and rough coats.

 Sow fresh seed; germination takes up to 15 weeks, sometimes more.

 Central and eastern China; not known in the wild

 USA Zones 7b to 11

Trithrinax acanthacoma

 12–15m (40–50ft) in the wild, invariably much less in cultivation, usually about 5.4m (18ft)

 1.8–3m (6–10ft)

 This moderately fast-growing palm needs well-drained soil and full sun in tropical, subtropical and warm-temperate areas. It is claimed to tolerate low temperatures down to -6°C (21.2°F), and can survive in considerably dry soil.

 Sow fresh seed; germination is both erratic and lengthy, often up to 30 weeks.

 Brazil and Argentina

 USA Zones 9 to 11

Buriti Palm, Spiny Fibre Palm

Deep-green or grey-green leaf segments, light green or bluish-green beneath, form stiff, fan-shaped leaves that are 90cm–1.2m (3–4ft) wide and borne on 60cm (2ft) leafstalks. Creamy-white flowers are followed by white fruits, about 18mm (¾in) across. The solitary trunk is cloaked in sharp spines, 7.5cm (3in) long, but clustered specimens with several trunks have been recorded.

Washingtonia filifera

(Washingtonia filamentosa)
American Cotton Palm, Californian Cotton Palm,
Californian Fan Palm, Californian Palm, Cotton Palm,
Desert Palm, Desert Fan Palm, Desert Washingtonia, Fan
Palm, Northern Washingtonia, Petticoat Palm

Yellow-green to grey-green, narrow, tapering segments form fan-shaped
leaves that are 1.8–2.4m (6–8ft) wide and borne on thorn-edged leafstalks
that are 1.8m (6ft) long. The leaf segments have thread-like fibres between
them. White, slightly fragrant flowers are followed by clusters of fruits that
mature to black or dark brown. The solitary trunk is often covered in
a layer of old leaves, but these are usually removed to reveal a narrowly fis-
sured grey or brown trunk 60–90cm (2–3ft) in diameter, sometimes more.

FACT FILE

 18m (60ft) in the wild, less in cultivation

 4.5–5.4m (15–18ft)

 This moderately fast-growing palm needs
well-drained but moisture-retentive soil
and full sun, in warm-temperate climates
or subtropical areas that are not excessively hot. Once established, it can survive
relatively dry soil.

 It is planted as a specimen palm or
street tree. It is often used as a house or
conservatory plant in temperate climates,
but is usually short-lived as a houseplant
as it requires high light intensity. It can
also be planted in large tubs in warm-
temperate and subtropical areas, when it
again needs a position in good light.

 Native Americans used the leaves for
making huts and baskets. The buds were
roasted for food.

 Sow fresh seed, which germinates quite
quickly, usually within 4–12 weeks,
sometimes more.

 California and western Arizona, northwest
Mexico

 USA Zones 7 to 11

A–Z PALMS

Washingtonia robusta

FACT FILE

 21–30m (70–100ft) in the wild, usually less in cultivation

 1.8–2.4m (6–8ft), sometimes slightly more

 Needs moisture-retentive but well-drained soil in full sun. Although it will survive periods of drought, it grows faster when given sufficient water. It is best suited to warm-temperate or subtropical areas as it is less cold tolerant than *Washingtonia filifera*. Once established, it can survive in relatively dry soil.

 Often used as a house or conservatory plant in temperate climates, and for planting in large tubs in warm-temperate and subtropical areas; position in good light. As a houseplant it is usually short-lived as it requires high light intensity.

 Sow fresh seed, which germinates quite quickly, usually within 4–12 weeks, sometimes more.

 Baja Peninsula in California, southwestern USA; the Mexican state of Sonora (also claimed to have originated in northwest Mexico)

 USA Zone 9b to 11

(Washingtonia sonora, Washingtonia gracilis)
Mexican Washington Palm, Mexican Washingtonia, Mexican Fan Palm, Skyduster, Southern Washingtonia, Thread Palm

This fast-growing palm can be readily distinguished from *Washingtonia filifera* by its taller, narrower stature. Deep-green leaf segments form fan-shaped leaves that are 90cm–1.5m (3–5ft) across and borne on 75cm–1.2m (2½–4ft) leafstalks. The edges of the leaves have thread-like fibres when young. White, slightly fragrant flowers are followed by black fruits. The solitary light-brown trunk is often clad in dead leaves.

Wodyetia bifurcata

Foxtail Palm

Dark-green leaflets form leaves 2.4–3m (8–10ft) long; they are borne on short leafstalks and have a bottle-brush or foxtail nature. Initially, the upper branches are upright, later arching and cascading at their ends. Yellowish-green flowers are followed by oval fruits that mature to a handsome orange or red. The solitary, light-grey to dull-white trunk is distinctively ringed.

A–Z PALMS

FACT FILE

 12–15m (40–50ft) in the wild, less in cultivation

 4.5–5.4m (15–18ft), sometimes slightly more

 Fertile, moisture-retentive soil and full sun are needed for fast growth; growth is much slower when in shade. It is tolerant of dry soil, but, again, growth is slower. It is at its best in tropical and subtropical areas. In warm-temperate climates it survives brief periods of low temperature.

 Its distinctive nature makes it ideal for planting as a specimen palm in a large area. It is also sometimes planted as a street tree. Indoors in temperate climates, it is best grown in a large container in a conservatory, where it needs good light. In tropical and subtropical regions it is often grown as an outdoor tub plant: position the container in full sun.

 Sow fresh seed, which usually germinates within 8–12 weeks, although up to a year has been recorded.

 Queensland, northeast Australia

 USA Zones 10 and 11

6
A–Z
of
cycads

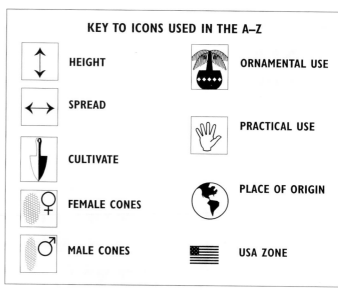

KEY TO ICONS USED IN THE A–Z

↕ HEIGHT	🌴 ORNAMENTAL USE
↔ SPREAD	
🔨 CULTIVATE	✋ PRACTICAL USE
♀ FEMALE CONES	🌍 PLACE OF ORIGIN
♂ MALE CONES	▦ USA ZONE

This A–Z of cycads describes and illustrates 18 species; others are featured in lists of cycads for specific climates and soils in Chapter 4. Some cycads have a palm-like nature and a distinctive trunk, while others are trunkless or have a fern-like appearance.

Each cycad's height and spread are indicated for the individual species, but these vary according to the plant's age and speed of growth, as well as damage caused by fires, grazing animals and land clearance. Cycads that have been damaged often produce further stems at their bases, and this misrepresents their normal growth. Many also have trunks that become branched. Remember, too, that the height and spread given in this chapter are for cycads growing in the wild; in cultivation, these are usually less, and even smaller when grown in large containers.

Damage is also caused through the ignorance of plant hunters, who, after seeing a plant in the wild, dig it up in the hope of transferring it to a garden or container. This is rarely successful and invariably results in the decimation of plants in the wild. Indeed, many cycads are now known only in botanic gardens, nurseries and private collections. Always buy plants from a reputable cycad nursery.

Increasing cycads by sowing seeds or detaching and rooting offsets is described in Chapter 3 (see pages 28–29). For home gardeners, detaching and rooting offsets is the best and easiest way to increase most cycads.

In the A–Z listings on the following pages, where common names are not given, they do not appear to exist.

Ceratozamia mexicana Mexican Horncone

Palm-like cycad with a trunk up to 1m (3½ft) high and 20cm (8in) in diameter. Arching leaves, about 1.5m (5ft) long and 75cm (30in) wide, are formed of 40–60 pairs of initially light-green leaflets that later become glossy, dark green. Each leaflet is about 38cm (15in) long and 18mm (¾in) wide. Sometimes, this cycad reveals a suckering nature.

FACT FILE

 1–1.8m (3½–6ft)   1.8–2.4m (6–8ft)

 Usually cylindrical, 25–35cm (10–14in) long and 8–12cm (3¼–4½in) across; dull grey

 Conical, 38–45cm (15–18in) long and about 7.5cm (3in) across; brown

 Fertile, moisture-retentive but well-drained soil are best, though in its native area it thrives in relatively dry soil. It flourishes in sun or light shade, but needs shelter from strong wind. It is warmth loving and best suited to warm-temperate regions, but tolerates cold for limited periods if the soil is well drained and relatively dry.

 Frequently planted in loose groups as an ornamental feature. Since it can live in low-intensity light, it is sometimes grown as a houseplant.

 Mexico   USA Zone 10

Ceratozamia robusta

Large, distinctive cycad with a tree-like stance, usually formed of an unbranched trunk 1–2.1m (3½–7ft) high and 20–30cm (8–12in) in diameter. Occasionally, it becomes branched as a result of injury. It has arched or curved leaves, which are 1.8–4m (6–13ft) long and 60–90cm (2–3ft) wide. Each bears 50–100 pairs of light-green leaflets, 25–40cm (10–16in) long and 25–36mm (1–1½in) across.

 3–3.6m (10–12ft)   3–3.6m (10–12ft), sometimes

 Horizontal or pendent, 25–40cm (10–16in) long and 10–15cm (4–6in) across; dark olive-green

 Cylindrical or conical, 30–40cm (12–16in) long, 5–7.5cm (2–3in) across; olive-green

 Needs fertile, moisture-retentive soil in light shade and an open position. It prefers tropical and subtropical conditions, but also grows well in warm-temperate areas. It tolerates wet soils.

 Suitable for large, ornamental areas.

 Southern Mexico, Belize, Guatemala   USA Zone 10

Cycas circinalis
False Sago, Fern Palm, Queen Sago, Sago Palm

FACT FILE

 6m (20ft), sometimes more

 3.6–4.5m (12–15ft), sometimes more

 Open type (where sporophylls are long and lax), 15–30cm (6–12in) long; brown

 Egg-like, somewhat cylindrical, 60–72cm (24–28in) long and 15–18cm (6–7in) across; yellowish-brown

 Sometimes deciduous or semi-deciduous in dry areas in the wild. To remain evergreen in cultivation, it needs moderately fertile, moisture-retentive soil and shelter from strong, cold winds. It tolerates moderate wind, drought and heat, and grows well in full sunlight or light shade.

 Edible sago can be extracted from the trunk. The foliage is used as decorative greenery for wreaths, and the seeds as emergency food.

 Southeast Asia   USA Zone 10b

This cycad belongs to a genus collectively known as Bread Palms, Coneheads and Funeral Palms. It has a tree-like nature, with a trunk up to about 6m (20ft) high and 25–38cm (10–15in) in diameter, with straight leaves 1.5–3m (5–10ft) long. Sometimes the trunk is branched. There are usually 15–20, glossy, glaucous-green leaves, each with up to 120 pairs of narrow leaflets, 20–30cm (8–12in) long and 12mm (½in) wide. It has dull-orange fruits.

Cycas media
Australian Nut Palm, Nut Palm

 4.5–6m (15–20ft), sometimes more

 2.4–3m (8–10ft)

 Open type, 20–38cm (8–15in) long; light, yellowish-brown fruits

 Egg-shaped to cylindrical, 15–30cm (6–12in) long and 8–15cm (3¼–6in) across; orange-brown

 Moisture-retentive and fertile soil suits it best. It likes warmth, but survives warm-temperate climates if the soil is relatively dry. It is said to tolerate heat and drought, and anything from full sun to light shade.

 The seeds are poisonous when raw, but have long been collected and roasted by aboriginal Australians in Queensland. The shells are removed and the kernel ground into flour.

 Western Australia   USA Zone 10

This cycad belongs to a genus collectively known as Bread Palms, Coneheads and Funeral Palms. It has an evergreen, palm- and tree-like nature, usually with an unbranched main stem, 90cm–3m (3–10ft) high and up to 30cm (12in) in diameter. The arching or curved, glaucous, dark-green leaves are up to 1.5m (5ft) long and 25cm (10in) wide. Each bears 60–100 pairs of narrow leaflets, about 20cm (8in) long and about 6mm (¼in) wide.

Cycas revoluta — Japanese Fern Palm, Japanese Sago Palm, Sago Palm

This belongs to a genus collectively known as Bread Palms, Coneheads and Funeral Palms. It has a tree-like stance, sometimes branched as it ages, and a trunk that is up to 1.8m (6ft) high and 90cm (3ft) in diameter. Old specimens are often 2–3 times this height (but this is an exception). The dark-green leaves, up to 1.5m (5ft) long and slightly more than 15cm (6in) wide, are initially upright, then spreading. They are slightly recurved or heavily arched at the ends. They are formed of narrow leaflets about 18cm (7in) long and 6mm (¼in) wide.

FACT FILE

 3–5.4m (10–18ft), sometimes more 2.4–3m (8–10ft)

 Closed type, 20–25cm (8–10in) long; yellow to orange-tan

 Cone-like to egg-shaped, 40–60cm (16–24in) long and 7.5–10cm (3–4in) across; yellow

 Adaptable cycad often exposed to salt spray in its native area, but grows more quickly in fertile, moisture-retentive soil and light shade. Tolerates cold for a limited time, but does best in temperate to warm-temperate regions.

 The foliage is used for funeral decoration and floral arrangements. The seeds are used as famine food. Both seeds and stems yield flour.

 It is used as a specimen in lawns, as a house or conservatory plant, or as indoor bonsai.

 Southern Japan USA Zones 9 and 10

Dioön edule — Chestnut Edule

Upright or slightly leaning tree-like cycad with a trunk that is 1.8–3m (6–10ft) long, sometimes more, and 20–40cm (8–16in) in diameter. Glaucous green, straight leaves, which are 90cm–1.3m (3–4¼ft) long and 18–20cm (7–8in) wide, are each formed of 80–120 pairs of leaflets, 6–12cm (2½–4¾in) long and about 12mm (½in) wide. In its native areas there is frequently variation between one group and another.

 1.8–3m (6–10ft) or more 1.8–2.1m (6–7ft) or more

 Egg-shaped, 25–27cm (10–10½in) long and 19–24cm (7½–9½in) across; white to grey

 Cylindrical, 18–20cm (7–8in) long and 6–7.5cm (2½–3in) across; white or brownish-grey

 Fertile, moisture-retentive soil encourages rapid growth. Thrives in partial shade, but tolerates full sun, drought, heat and salt-laden wind. Grows well in warm-temperate regions but is said to tolerate cold and a limited amount of frost.

 The seeds have a high starch content and were earlier used to produce flour. An extract from the seeds was used in Mexico and Central America to treat neuralgia.

 Mexico and Central America USA Zone 10

Dioön mejiae

FACT FILE

 6–9m (20–30ft)

 2.4–4.5m (8–15ft)

 Egg-shaped, 30–45cm (12–18in) long and 25–35cm (10–14in) across; tan-coloured

 Cylindrical, 25–45cm (10–18in) long and about 10cm (4in) across; tan-coloured

 Fertile, moisture-retentive soil and warmth encourage rapid growth. Grows well in sun or light shade, and tolerates drought, cool temperatures and salt-laden wind. It grows well in warm-temperate regions.

 Natives of Honduras have used the seeds to produce flour, while leaves have been used to decorate churches and in funeral wreaths.

 It creates an attractive feature in large lawns, but avoid positioning plants close together as their outlines will be spoiled.

 Mexico and Honduras

USA Zone 10

A large, tree-like cycad, it has stems up to 6m (20ft) or more high and 15–35cm (6–14in) in diameter. The stiff, straight, glaucous green leaves are 1–1.8m (3½–6ft) long and 32cm (13in) wide, each formed of 75–100 pairs of leaflets, 15–17cm (6–6½in) long and about 12mm (½in) wide.

 10.5m (35ft), sometimes slightly more; claims of 15m (50ft) high have been made

 3–3.6m (10–12ft), sometimes more

 Cylindrical to egg-shaped, 35–50cm (14–20in) long and 25cm (10in) across; tan with a covering of downy hairs

 Cylindrical to egg-shaped, 20–50cm (8–20in) long and 10–13cm (4–5in) across; tan and with a covering of downy hairs

 Fertile, moisture-retentive soil and warmth encourages rapid growth. Grows well in sun or shade. It prefers hot areas, but also grows well in warm-temperate regions.

 It is an attractive cycad for ornamental planting, but is usually too high for widespread use, unless in large areas.

 The seeds have been used to produce flour, and the sap for chewing gum. The leaves are used for decoration.

 Mexico

USA Zone 10

Dioön spinulosum

This large, tree-like cycad has stems claimed to be 7.5m (25ft) or more high and 18–25cm (7–10in) wide. The grey-green, glaucous, arching leaves are 1.5–1.8m (5–6ft) long and 30–40cm (12–16in) wide, each formed of 80 to more than 100 pairs of leaflets, 15–20cm (6–8in) long and about 12mm (½in) wide.

Encephalartos altensteinii Bread Tree, Prickly Cycad

This easily grown, fast-growing, tree-like cycad has an erect trunk, up to 5m (16½ft) high and 25–35cm (10–14in) in diameter. The usually straight, bright-green or yellowish leaves are 1.5–2.1m (5–7ft) long and 35cm (14in) wide. Each leaf has 100 or more pairs of leaflets, about 13cm (5in) long and 18–25mm (¾–1in) wide.

FACT FILE

 5.4m (18ft), sometimes more

 3–3.6m (10–12ft), sometimes more

 ♀ Cylindrical to egg-shaped, 40–50cm (16–20in) long and 20–30cm (8–12in) across; greenish-yellow to golden-yellow

 ♂ Somewhat cylindrical, 40–50cm (16–20in) long and 12–15cm (4½–6in) across; greenish-yellow to golden-yellow

 Fertile, moisture-retentive soil ensures rapid growth. It grows in both shade and full sun, tolerates cool areas and strong wind, but grows best in temperate to warm-temperate regions.

 Often planted as a landscape feature, or grown as a tub plant.

 South Africa USA Zones 9 and 10

Encephalartos eugene-maraisii Waterberg Cycad

This distinctive, ornamental, tree-like cycad has a trunk that is initially upright, but later sometimes leaning. It is up to 1.8–2.1m (6–7ft) high and 30–40cm (12–16in) in diameter. It often has a suckering and clump-forming nature. Its light-grey or glaucous green leaves are eventually 1–1.5m (3½–5ft) long and 10cm (4in) wide. The leaflets are 15–20cm (6–8in) long and about 12mm (½in) wide.

 3–3.6m (10–12ft), sometimes more

 1.5–2.4m (5–8ft), sometimes more and forming large clumps

 ♀ Somewhat egg-shaped, 30–50cm (12–20in) long and 15–20cm (6–8in) across; maroon or dark brownish-red

 ♂ Spindle-like, 23–40cm (9–16in) long and 6–8cm (2½–3½in) across; maroon or dark brownish-red

 Fertile, moisture-retentive soil and a warm, wind-sheltered position suit it best. Tolerates full sun, drought and both heat and cold. It grows best in temperate to warm-temperate regions.

 Often grown as an ornamental feature.

 South Africa USA Zones 9 and 10

A–Z CYCADS

Encephalartos friderici-guilielmii Kaiser's Cycad, Woolly Cycad

FACT FILE

 4m (13ft), or slightly more

 1.8–3m (6–10ft), sometimes more, especially when sucking and forming a large clump

 Barrel-like, 25–30cm (10–12in) long and 15–20cm (6–8in) across; yellow, but covered with a yellowish-grey or brownish wool; yellow or orange fruits

 Somewhat cylindrical, 20–40cm (8–16in) long and 6–10cm (2½–4in) across; brownish wool

 Well-drained but moisture-retentive soil and full sun are needed. It tolerates drought and heat, as well as cold and wind, but grows best in temperate to warm-temperate regions.

 South Africa USA Zones 9 and 10

This distinctive, tree-like cycad has a trunk 3–3.6m (10–12ft) high and 35–60cm (14–24in) in diameter. Sometimes it has a clump-forming or suckering nature. The straight or slightly curved, mid-green or glaucous-green leaves have woolly undersides when young, and are 1–1.5m (3½–5ft) long and 18–20cm (7–8in) wide. The leaflets are 10–17cm (4–6½in) long and 6mm (¼in) wide, or slightly more.

 2.1–3m (7–10ft)

 1.3–1.8m (4½–6ft), sometimes more

 Egg-shaped, 20–35cm (8–14in) long and 15–20cm (6–8in) across; yellowish, but covered with brown wool; orange fruits. Cultivated plants seldom produce cones, male or female

 Somewhat cylindrical, 27–30cm (11–12in) long, 15–17cm (6–6½in) across; brown wool

 Needs fertile, moisture-retentive soil and full sun.

 Swaziland and South Africa USA Zones 9 and 10

Encephalartos heenanii Woolly Cycad

This distinctive, tree-like cycad has a trunk about 2.1m (7ft) high and 25–35cm (10–14in) in diameter. It has a suckering nature. The upper sides of the leaves, 1–1.3m (3½–4½ft) long and 15–20cm (6–8in) wide, are covered in golden-brown wool. The leaflets are 12–15cm (4½–6in) long and about 18mm (¾in) wide.

Encephalartos longifolius Suurberg Cycad

This tree-like cycad's trunk is 2.7–3.6m (9–12ft) high and 30–45cm (12–18in) in diameter. Sometimes it has a suckering nature. The arched or curved, blue-grey leaves are 1–1.8m (3½–6ft) long and 18–23cm (7–9in) wide. Each leaf is formed of leaflets 15–20cm (6–8in) long and about 25mm (1in) wide.

FACT FILE

 3–3.6m (10–12ft), sometimes more

 2.1–3m (7–10ft), sometimes more

 Egg-shaped, 50–60cm (20–24in) long and 30–40cm (12–16in) across; greenish-brown

 Somewhat cylindrical, 40–60cm (16–24in) long and 14–20cm (5½–8in) across; greenish-brown

 In its native area it often grows in well-drained scrubland, but in cultivation it thrives in fertile, moisture-retentive but well-drained soil. Tolerates heat, full sun, drought, cold areas and strong wind, but grows best in temperate to warm-temperate regions. It is claimed to tolerate slight frost.

 Widely grown as an ornamental cycad and forms a moderately dominant feature.

 South Africa

 USA Zones 9 and 10

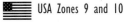 **A–Z CYCADS**

Encephalartos transvenosus

Modjadji Cycad, Modjadji Palm

This tall, tree-like cycad usually has an unbranched trunk, 4.5–7.5m (15–25ft) high and 40–60cm (16–24in) in diameter. It has a suckering nature, while stems become branched when they are damaged. Sometimes it is taller, with heights of 12m (40ft) being recorded. The straight or arching, dark-green or blue-green leaves are 1.5–2.4m (5–8ft) long and 20–40cm (8–16in) wide. Each is formed of leaflets 10–20cm (4–8in) long and about 42mm (1¾in) wide.

 Up to 9m (30ft), sometimes more

 3–4.5m (10–15ft), sometimes more

 Egg-shaped, 50–82cm (20–32in) long and 20–30cm (8–12in) across; golden-brown and slightly woolly. Bears yellow or red fruits

 Somewhat cylindrical, 30–60cm (12–24in) long and 13–15cm (5–6in) across; golden-brown

 Take care not to crowd it. For rapid growth, plant in fertile, well-drained but moisture-retentive soil in light shade or full sun.
It tolerates heat, drought, wet soil, cold and strong wind, but grows best in temperate to warm-temperate regions. It is claimed to tolerate slight frost.

 South Africa

USA Zones 9 and 10

Lepidozamia hopei

FACT FILE

 Up to 15m (50ft), sometimes slightly more

 3–4.5m (10–15ft), sometimes slightly more

 Egg-shaped, 40–82cm (16–32in) long and 20–30cm (8–12in) across; grey-green. Bears bright red fruits

 Somewhat cylindrical, 40–72cm (16–28in) long and 10–13cm (4–5in) wide; brown

 Fertile, moisture-retentive soil and a warm, wind-sheltered position suit it best, but it is known to survive cool areas and slight frost. Tolerates shade and strong wind. Ideal for subtropical to tropical regions, but also grows in warm-temperate regions.

 Superb as an ornamental cycad, it used to be planted as an avenue tree.

 Northeast Queensland, Australia

USA Zone 10

Perhaps the tallest cycad, it has a tree-like nature. Its trunk is up to 15m (50ft) high and about 1.5m (5ft) in diameter at its base. Occasionally, it is branched, especially if it has been damaged. The initially straight and spreading – later arched or curved – glossy, dark-green leaves are 1.8–3m (6–10ft) long and 40–82cm (16–32in) wide. Each bears 80–100 pairs of leaflets, 20–40cm (8–16in) long and about 25mm (1in) wide.

 6–7.5m (20–25ft), sometimes more

 3–5.4m (10–18ft), sometimes less

 Egg-shaped, 40–90cm (16–36in) long and 25–35cm (10–14in) across; bright salmon-red interior; bright red fruits

 Somewhat cylindrical, 40–75cm (16–30in) long and 10–12cm (4–4½in) across; cream-coloured

 Plant in fertile, moisture-retentive soil and a warm, wind-sheltered position, although it is known to survive cool areas, slight frost and strong wind. It grows best in warm-temperate regions and tolerates full sun or shade.

 Superb as an ornamental cycad, it used to be planted as an avenue tree.

 New South Wales to Queensland, Australia

 USA Zone 10

Lepidozamia peroffskyana

This upright, fast-growing cycad has a tree-like nature. Its trunk is approximately 6m (20ft) high and 30–60cm (1–2ft) in diameter at its base; sometimes it is branched as a result of damage. The graceful, arching, glossy dark-green leaves are 1.8–3m (6–10ft) long and 40–50cm (16–20in) wide. Young leaves are often shaded with bronze. Each leaf produces 70–125 pairs of leaflets, 10–30cm (4–12in) long and about 12mm (½in) wide.

Macrozamia communis Burrawong

This fast-growing cycad develops stems that are 1–2.1m (3½–7ft) high and 30–60cm (1–2ft) wide. The dull, dark-green, graceful, arching leaves are up to about 1.8m (6ft) long and 45cm (18in) wide. Each has 70–120 pairs of leaflets, up to 35cm (14in) long and 12mm (½in) wide.

FACT FILE

 2.4m (8ft), sometimes slightly more

 3–3.6m (10–12ft), sometimes slightly more

 Cylindrical, 20–45cm (8–18in) and 10–20cm (4–8in) across; glaucous green; bright red fruits

 Cylindrical, 20–45cm (8–18in) long and 8–12cm (3½–4½in) across; glaucous green

 Fertile, moisture-retentive but well-drained soil and partial shade encourage rapid growth. Flourishes in warmth, but tolerates temperate and warm-temperate areas. Survives strong, salt-laden wind and tolerates slight frost or full sun.

 Widely used in landscape planting and large gardens.

 New South Wales, Australia USA Zones 9 and 10

Zamia floridana

Conti, Conti-hateka, Coonti, Coontie, Comptie, Florida Arrowroot, Indian Bread Root, Koonti, Seminole-bread

Also known as *Zamia integrifolia*, it has a low-growing nature, with stems 20–25cm (8–10in) high and about 7.5cm (3in) wide. The arched or spreading, glossy and medium- to dark-green leaves are 45–90cm (1½–3ft) long and about 15cm (6in) wide. Every leaf is formed of 10–25 pairs of leaflets, each about 7.5cm (3in) long and 12mm (½in) wide, sometimes less.

 75–90cm (2½–3ft) 1.2–1.5m (4–5ft), sometimes more

 Cylindrical, 12–15cm (4½–6in) long and about 5cm (2in) across; dark brownish-red, with orange fruits

 Cylindrical to cone-like, 6–10cm (2½–4in) long and about 25mm (1in) across; reddish-brown

 Fertile, moisture-retentive but well-drained soil and warmth produce fast growth, but the cycad does survive in warm-temperate climates. Ensure it is not exposed to frost.

 Starch from the stem was eaten by Native Americans, and sold as Florida Arrowroot.

 Southern Georgia and Florida Keys, USA USA Zones 9 and 10

Plant Hardiness Zones

To enable gardeners in the United States of America to assess which plants grow in particular regions, the country is divided into 11 Plant Hardiness Zones that encompass territories from Canada through to very warm areas such as Honolulu in Hawaii. Most zones are divided into 'a' (cooler parts) and 'b' (warmer parts) to reflect variations within zones.

These zones are based on 10°F differences in the average annual minimum temperatures and have been produced by the United States Department of Agriculture (USDA). These temperature zones range from 1 to 11, but only those from 5 to 11 concern palms and cycads. Zone 11, shown as an inset, encompasses Honolulu, Hawaii and parts of Mexico that experience minimum average temperatures of 4.5°C (40°F) and above, and are free of frost throughout the year.

These zones have their critics, largely because they do not consider micro-climates that reflect the nature of soils, wind-chill factors, sunlight levels, humidity, altitude and rainfall. Nevertheless, they do give clues to the areas in which specific palms and cycads can be grown. If you are doubtful about the hardiness of a particular palm or cycad in your area, visit a local garden centre or plant specialist.

To create a detailed picture of the suitability of areas, the following chart indicates average annual minimum temperatures for each zone.

USDA PLANT HARDINESS MAP

AVERAGE ANNUAL MINIMUM TEMPERATURES

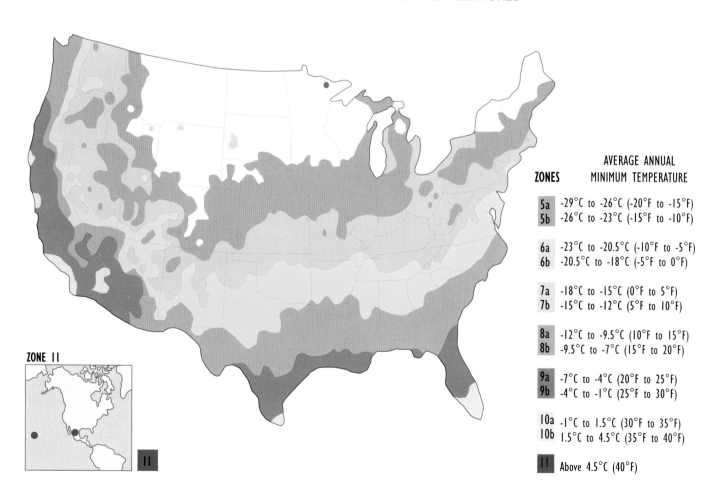

ZONE 11

ZONES	AVERAGE ANNUAL MINIMUM TEMPERATURE
5a	-29°C to -26°C (-20°F to -15°F)
5b	-26°C to -23°C (-15°F to -10°F)
6a	-23°C to -20.5°C (-10°F to -5°F)
6b	-20.5°C to -18°C (-5°F to 0°F)
7a	-18°C to -15°C (0°F to 5°F)
7b	-15°C to -12°C (5°F to 10°F)
8a	-12°C to -9.5°C (10°F to 15°F)
8b	-9.5°C to -7°C (15°F to 20°F)
9a	-7°C to -4°C (20°F to 25°F)
9b	-4°C to -1°C (25°F to 30°F)
10a	-1°C to 1.5°C (30°F to 35°F)
10b	1.5°C to 4.5°C (35°F to 40°F)
11	Above 4.5°C (40°F)

EUROPEAN TEMPERATURE ZONES

A temperature zone guide for Europe is useful but not completely satisfactory as, like the USDA guide for North America (opposite), it ignores microclimates. Nonetheless, this chart provides a general guide. It encompasses five temperature zones, which equate to those applicable in North America. Gardeners in the UK, for example, need to look mainly for palms that grow in USA Zones 8 and 9.

USA ZONE	AVERAGE ANNUAL MINIMUM TEMPERATURE	
6	-23°C to -18°C	(-10°F to 0°F)
7	-18°C to -12°C	(0°F to 10°F)
8	-12°C to -6.5°C	(10°F to 20°F)
9	-6.5°C to -1°C	(20°F to 30°F)
10	-1°C to 4.5°C	(30°F to 40°F)

AUSTRALIAN TEMPERATURE ZONES

The Australian continent has been divided into seven temperature zones that encompass American Zones of Hardiness 7b to 11. The map shows these two temperature zone classifications in comparison with each other, together with the average annual lowest temperatures in Australia. By checking with the recommended temperatures suggested for palms and cycads in North America, it is possible to judge the best possible area in Australia.

Many palms grow well in temperatures higher than those that equate to USDA Zone 11, such as the temperatures experienced in Australian Zones 6 and 7. For these zones, the warmth-loving palms that grow in USDA Zone 11 should be successful.

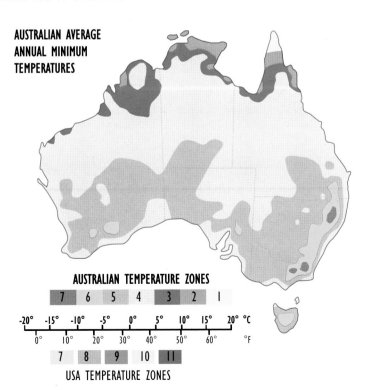

AUSTRALIAN AVERAGE ANNUAL MINIMUM TEMPERATURES

AUSTRALIAN TEMPERATURE ZONES
7 6 5 4 3 2 1

-20° -15° -10° -5° 0° 5° 10° 15° 20° °C
0° 10° 20° 30° 40° 50° 60° °F

7 8 9 10 11
USA TEMPERATURE ZONES

Glossary

Acaricide Chemical spray or dust to kill mites, such as red spider mites

Acid Soil/compost with pH below 7.0

Adventitious roots see Aerial roots

Aerial roots Roots arising from a stem above compost level

Alkaline Soil/compost with pH above 7.0

Anther Pollen-bearing part of a stamen, the male part of a flower

Aphids Also known as greenfly, they cluster on stems, shoots, etc., sucking sap and causing damage

Arborescent Having a tree-like nature

Asexual reproduction Propagation by vegetative rather than sexual means

Axil Junction and angle between leaf and stem

Axillary Borne in an axil

Blade The expanded part of a leaf

Bloom (1) flower; (2) powdery white covering

Bole The trunk of a tree or palm

Bottom heat Warmth at the base of a cutting when propagating

Bud Tightly packed, immature shoot or flower

Calcareous Grows in limy or chalky soil

Calcicole Plant that likes lime

Calcifuge Plant that dislikes lime

Callus Hard and corky layer that develops over a cut or wound, usually resulting in a raised surface, especially around the tissue's edges

Cambium Thin layer of cell tissue found just under the bark, which initiates growth; absent in palms and cycads

Cane-type palm Having reed-like stems that look like bamboo canes when mature, e.g. *Chamaedorea seifrizii*

Clustered Clumping, with several stems

Cold frame Glazed, wooden or concrete-sided framework in which small plants are protected from excessive cold and wet weather; traditionally unheated with sides 23–30cm (9–12in) high, sometimes slightly higher for tall plants

Compost (1) mixture of friable loam, sharp sand, peat and fertilizers in which plants in pots and other containers are grown; (2) mixture of vegetable material (grass cuttings and vegetable waste) that has been encouraged to decay and is later dug into the soil or spread over the surface of soil to form a mulch – best known as garden compost

Compound leaf Leaf formed of two or more leaflets, which do not have buds in the junctions between leaflet and stem; all true leaves have buds in their leaf axils

Cone Structure formed of sporophylls, bearing the reproductive organs

Coralloid Type of root that resembles coral in structure and has a blue-green colour

Crown Upper part of a tree, where branches spread out from the trunk

Crownshaft Term used with some pinnate-leaved palms to define the cylindrical or tubular shaft above the woody part of a trunk; it is formed of tightly packed leaf bases

Cultivar Plant produced in cultivation and indicating a 'cultivated variety'. Earlier, all variations, whether produced naturally in the wild or in cultivation, were known as 'varieties'. The term has been used by gardeners for decades and is still frequently seen. To many gardeners 'variety' is less formal than 'cultivar'

Cycad Popular term for members of the *Cycadaceae*, a group of primitive plants belonging to Gymnosperms and representing one of the earliest groups of seed-bearing plants. Their flowers are borne in cone-like structures; there are both male and female cones. Mainly native to tropical and subtropical regions, although some tolerate warm-temperate regions

Deciduous Shrub or tree that sheds its leaves naturally at the end of its growing season, usually autumn and early winter, and produces a fresh array in spring. Most palms and cycads are evergreen; in the wild some cycads become deciduous or semi-deciduous when in dry soil and a low temperature

Dibber Blunt-ended or slightly pointed tool (usually made of wood) used for making holes in compost or soil into which the roots of seedlings or plants are inserted; those used for inserting seedlings are usually 10–13cm (4–5in) long, whereas those used in a garden for planting cabbages and other brassicas are about 25cm (10in) long and often have a D-shaped or T-shaped handle

Dioecious Having single-sexed flowers on separate plants

Down Fine, soft hairs on the leaves and fruits of some plants

Epiphyte Plant that grows in a non-parasitic form on another

Evergreen Shrub or tree that retains its leaves throughout the year, appearing to be 'evergreen' though it is continually shedding some leaves while producing new ones. Some evergreens native to warm areas become semi-evergreen or lose all their leaves when in a cool, temperate climate

Fan-type palm 'Palmate' plant with fronds split into main segments that radiate from a point where they are collectively attached to a leaf-stalk, e.g. *Chamaerops humilis*

Feather-type palm Having fronds that are divided on either side of the midrib to create an impression of many leaflets, e.g. *Howea belmoreana*, and *Howea forsteriana*

Fishtail-type palm Having leaflets resembling fishtails, e.g. *Caryota mitis*

Frond A leaf of a palm or fern

Fungicide Chemical used to control fungal diseases

Genus Group of plants with similar botanical characteristics; within a genus are one or more species, each with slightly different characteristics

Germination Process that occurs in a seed when given adequate moisture, air and warmth. The seed-coat ruptures and a seed-leaf (or leaves) grows upward and toward the light. At the same time, a root develops and grows downward. To most gardeners, germination is when they see seed-leaves appearing through the surface of compost or soil

Glabrous Smooth, without hairs or other coverings

Glaucous Having a bluish-green colour, often accompanied by a powdery covering

Growing point Terminal part of a shoot that initiates growth

Gymnosperms Belonging to one of the two divisions of the seed-bearing plants and characterized by ovules that sit naked on flattened, and scale-like carpels arranged in spikes (known as strobili)

Hardy Plant that can be left outside during winter in temperate climates

Humidity Amount of moisture in the atmosphere; the higher the temperature, the more moisture air can retain

Inflorescence The flowering part of a plant

Insecticide Chemical used to kill insects

Juvenile foliage Young leaves of a tree; may differ from adult foliage

Lamina Expanded part of a leaf

Lanceolate Lance-shaped; usually used to describe the shape of a leaf

Leaf axil Junction between leaf and stem, or leaflet and leaf-stem

Leaflet Separate blade of a compound leaf; it does not have a bud in its axil; there are usually many leaflets on a compound leaf

Loam Mixture of sand, clay, silt and decomposed organic material

Mist-spraying Use of a sprayer to create a fine mist of clean water around plants to increase humidity

Offset Shoot arising from the base of a trunk or stem

Open-type Female cone of a cycad in which sporophylls are long and lax

Ovule Female part of a flower that becomes a seed after fertilization

Palm Member of the *Palmae* and mostly native to the tropics and subtropics; some can grow outdoors in warm-temperate regions

Palmate Hand- or fan-shaped leaf

Peat Partly decomposed vegetable material, usually acidic, often used in potting and seed composts; cutting this material from peat beds destroys the environments of many birds, animals and insects

Pesticide Chemical compound for killing insects and other pests

Petiole Leafstalk

Petiolule Stalk that attaches a leaflet to a leafstalk

pH Logarithmic scale used to define the acidity or alkalinity of soil or compost; neutral is 7.0, with figures above indicating increasing alkalinity, and those below, increasing acidity

Pinnate Feather-shaped leaf

Plumose Having a feather-like nature; with palms it refers to leaves that are orientated in different directions to create this clustered appearance

Propagation Raising of new plants

Seed compost Type of compost, usually formed of friable loam, sharp sand and peat, that provides seeds with the essentials for germination

Sharp sand Type of sand (sometimes known as concreting sand) with a coarse, gritty nature that allows air to penetrate compost and excess moisture to drain away

Species Group of plants that breed together and have the same characteristics. Species belong to a genus that can be formed of one or more species; within a species, there may be several cultivars

Sporophyll Leaf-like structure of a cone that bears ovules, sporangia or pollen capsules

Stigma Female parts of a flower that receive the pollen from the male part

Strobile A cone, the spore-bearing structure

Sucker Shoot arising from the base of a stem or the roots, usually from below soil level

Systemic Insecticide or fungicide that can enter a plant's tissue and provide protection against pests and diseases

Tender Plant in a temperate climate that cannot survive winter outdoors

Variety See cultivar

Vegetative propagation Method of increasing plants, including the division of roots, layering and taking cuttings

Index of common names

Index of scientific names

Photographic credits   All photographs by **Toby Spanner,** except those listed below:

Armstrong pages: 3 bottom left; 14 bottom left. **Australia National Botanical Gardens** pages: 12 left; 62; 144 bottom right; 115 top. **Gallo** pages: 1; 4–5; 6; 44. **Garden Picture Library** pages: 21; 24 right; 50; 68; 75. **Garden World Images** pages: 2–3; 9; 10 bottom left and right; 11 middle right; 13 right; 14 top right and bottom right; 15 bottom right; 16 bottom left; 17 bottom right; 25 top; 43; 51 left; 58; 59; 61; 70; 74; 78; 82; 84; 86; 87; 95; 100 top; 101 top; 107; 112; 115; 116; 117; 119; 122; 127; 130; 132; 134; 140; 142; 145 bottom; 147 top; 149 top and bottom. **New Holland Picture Library** pages:10 top left; 27 left; 31; 33. **Peter McHoy** pages: 8 middle right; 36; 145 top. **Photos Horticultural** pages: 69; 85; 104. **Science Photo** pages: 8 left and middle right; 30; 31; 40 top and bottom; 51 right; 56; 81; 99 top; 103; 126; 131; 139. **The Palm Centre** pages: 100 bottom; 135; 147 bottom.